ISLAND BUSH PILOT:

Founder of San Juan Airlines

By Roy Franklin

Copyright © 2006
by Roy Franklin

Published by Avian Ridge Books
53 Avian Ridge Lane
Friday Harbor, WA 98250

ISBN #0-9674369-4-X

Library of Congress Cataloging-in-Publication Data are available from the publisher on request.

Printed and bound in the U.S.A. by Booksurge

To my wife Margaret Ann.
You have been gone 4 years, my love. 56
years together, 5 children, 9 grandchildren, 2 great
grandchildren, and a commuter airline.
I will love you forever.

CONTENTS

Acknowledgments

Acknowledgments

After selling the Air Service in 1979 it was the surviving old-timers who caused me to write this book. I was asked to give a talk on both Orcas and San Juan Islands, so I did. I was amazed at how many old-timers came up after the talks and said, "you've got to put those old stories into print before they are all lost."

So that is what I'm attempting to do.

I hope my old friends are not disappointed—telling stories is one thing, writing a book is something else. If it hadn't been for former Orcas Islanders, Robert Hall and his wife, Mona, and a San Juan Islander, John Geyman and his patient spouse, Gene, and my family, I probably would have struck out in the final inning. In finally bringing this book to publication, I am indebted to Bruce Conway of Lightwatcher Publishing in Friday Harbor for his help, including book design, layout and graphics, and to Virginia Gessner for her skillful preparation of the entire manuscript.

Pathway to the Stars

An aircraft mechanic/pilot, Frank Gunneman, wrote this many years ago. It was published in the *Business and Commercial Aviation* magazine.

On the cool blue of the sky… in and out among the clouds like a shadow on the wind… my craft will drift.
Alive am I.
Joyous, jubilant… with the knowledge… with the wonder… that I can fly.
The wings that carry me are like two outstretched arms that flex beneath the sun… their metal skin reflecting light beams that seem to dance in a golden swirl of unfiltered beauty.
But eventually my craft must land; it must leave this wonderland above the clouds and return me to that other world.
Yet in returning me to the common path and trials of life, I shall then know… that to fly… is but to taste a sample of the beauty above the clouds…
And that man was only meant in life to stop a few short moments on the pathway to the stars.

If you have ever tried to beat off frozen snow from an airplane while a doctor is waiting, trying to keep someone alive, you don't have to be a genius to know the first building you better build is an aircraft hangar.

If you have ever had your heart slamming against your rib cage while you feel your way down at seventy miles per hour onto a black and unlighted cow pasture, there will be no doubt as to the value of runway lights.

If you have ever worked all night on a sick engine with frozen fingers and lockjaw from holding a flashlight in your mouth, you will automatically be making plans for a lighted and heated aircraft maintenance building.

If you have ever started out the first flight of the day with fuel gauges bobbing on empty and the closest fuel miles away across the waters on the mainland, you know you will mortgage your soul for a local fueling facility.

If you have tried to the last ounce of your strength and resolve to maintain an on-time flight schedule with aircraft mired axle-deep in mud or a blown tire from frozen ruts, or watched your few and precious passengers step in cow pies, you will know about drainage, hard-surfaced runways, and airfields that are for airplanes and people and not cattle.

And finally if you have ever experienced the joy of parents greeting a well and happy child when only nights before the same child was near death; seen the dignity and courage of a senior citizen on his last ride; experienced the thrill and wonderment of a first airplane rider, young or old—then you will begin to understand how it was with us.

—Roy Franklin

As quoted in *Commuter Airlines of the United States,* Edited by R.E.G. Davies and I. E. Quastler, Smithsonian Institute Press, 1995, p. 180

CHAPTER 1

A Farm Boy and Uncle James

For me, being just a five-year-old kid, it was almost impossible to visualize. This ancient, frail old man with his shaking hands and barely audible voice, shuffling across the kitchen floor to examine the stack of wood my Dad and I had brought in. And this little mite of a withered old lady, humming a tuneless tune and not seeming to even see us as she slowly examined each vegetable my Mom had sent. Ride like the wind? Crack shot with a rifle? Set hearts aflutter as they whirled around the dance floor? Good Lord! My Dad must have been nipping the hard cider again to have dreamed up such a story as that!

But then there were those things in the pantry? My Dad said not to touch anything and I didn't but it was a terrible trial to keep my hands back. Especially from the old bullet mold or those cans of Dupont rifle powder with the picture of the hunter on the label, or that beat-up old saddle canteen. Man oh man, those were real items, things that could send a boy's imagination off to the outer limits of the wild frontier.

Driving back to our farm my Dad let me sit on his lap and steer. I wasn't half bad for a kid but on this day he had to speak sharply several times or I'd of ditched the old Chevy for sure. My Dad didn't ask me where my mind was, he seemed to know. His big warm hands gently enclosed my hands on the wheel and he began to talk about the old folks.

Dad said Aunt Annie was an orphan. Somewhere around Civil War time and as a young girl, she had been adopted by my Mom's people. When Annie was grown-up she married James Clayton, who was also an orphan and a War veteran.

I had never heard of so many kids being orphans, but my Dad said back in those days of fevers and pestilence there were lots of kids without moms and dads.

When my Mom's family moved West, Annie and her husband followed. James and Annie Clayton never had children. We were all the family they ever had. To us kids, and eventually to our whole family, they became Uncle James and Aunt Annie.

Now they were real old and the family was helping them out.

Yeah, well this was all kind of interesting but what I wanted to know about was Uncle James riding like the wind—and what about the bullet mold and that old canteen? Did my Dad think arrows or bullets made the dents on the canteen and was Uncle James wounded?

My Dad laughed and said he doubted it, but if Uncle James was not so old he surely could have told me some great adventure stories. Uncle James at 14 years old and during the Civil War had been a drummer boy with the rebel cavalry. WOW!

My Dad said when Uncle James was younger he flowed with a horse like he was glued to him and he was an excellent rifle shot.

After my Dad had told me about all these things, visits to Uncle James and Aunt Annie's were much more interesting. I couldn't help staring at the old man, visualizing him young and brave---riding at the head of wild, thundering cavalry charges--- cannon blasts and rifle fire everywhere; and the rebel yell!

But now it was different. Uncle James and Aunt Annie were dead. Died within days of each other. My Dad and Mom were in the house with all the other grown-up relatives discussing the sale of the place and the paying off of the doctor bills, and all that stuff. I wondered where the old folks had gone. Everybody said they were dead but my Mom said they had gone to heaven and would be born again.

When I heard the men say my Dad could have the hunting equipment if he liked, I held my breath. My Dad turned and looked at me with kind of a twinkle in his eyes and said, "That will be alright!" For some reason the men all chuckled.

That day in the house while everyone was talking, it thundered. In the silence that followed, I said, "Uncle James is born again and riding hell for leather across heaven in a cavalry charge?" Some thought it kind of funny but there were others who thought I ought to have my mouth washed out with soap. I was invited to go outside and play.

When the Claytons had gotten old they had sold their farm and moved to a town lot in the little village of Ferndale.

There was one place on their lot I had not explored and that was the carriage barn. From the outside it was an attractive building. Not large as barns go but probably plenty big for several horses, a carriage, hay storage, etc. Now it was all locked up, dark and cobwebby. My Dad said, "Stay out of there--- it hasn't been used for years--- there's nothing left in there."

Having been kicked out of the house, the barn now became the center of my attention. The more I studied it the more I was sure it held the key to high adventure! I could just imagine Uncle James's uniform and rifle, saddle and bridle all hanging on the wall (probably an arrow still sticking in the crown of the old felt hat).

No one was looking, the grownups were all in the house, the carriage barn was drawing me like a magnet. A back window was gone so I crawled through. Inside… it was so spooky and silent I scarcely dared breathe. I was in the old horse stall area. The light was dim and shadowy. With little prickles of fear running up and down my back I slowly made my way through the cobwebs to the driveway, the center of the barn. There was nothing there; no carriage, no harness, no saddles, no nothing.

Slowly, disappointedly, fearfully, I started climbing the ladder to the hay loft over the horse stable. As my eyes came above the flooring, I froze, literally transfixed. Through a crack in the barn wall shone a brilliant shaft of sunlight… and in that shaft of light the cobwebs gleaned like a beautiful halo… and in that halo hung Uncle James's cavalry saddle!

Many years later, climbing skyward in our fighter planes, through fleecy white clouds and halos of brilliant sunshine, I thought again of Uncle James. I was a member of Uncle Sam's 'aerial-cavalry.' The name of our flight was 'Rebel Flight.' As we formed into 'trail', diving, zooming, weaving through the fantastic cloud canyons of the sky, I found myself shouting with sheer joy. I swear my voice was not alone.

CHAPTER 2

Navy Pilot to Flight Instructor

During the War I had felt lucky to be flying single-engined fighters. Now, faced with trying to find my nitch in civilian aviation, I found myself envying the bomber-boys and their many hours of multi-engined experience. So I figured I had to get a job instructing for one of the GI flight schools. That or crop-dusting were about the only other alternatives.

To be eligible for employment with one of the flight schools after World War II, one needed a flight instructor's license. Not having the required rating but determined to stay with aviation, I signed up for the course with a GI flight school. The outfit was called Western Washington Aviation and it was based at the Bellingham Airport.

All kinds of things happened on my first day at the flight school. First, I ended up with a new name. My first name, Roy, was the same as my Dad's name. At home and while growing up, I'd been known by my middle name, Vincent, or Vince. My Mother was the only one who called me Vincent and she only did that when she was mad at me.

Now as I waited in Western Washington's flight office for the lady to check over my application, I had time to study my immediate surroundings. At the far end of the room several flight instructors and students were at a blackboard discussing flight maneuvers. Just by sight it was hard to tell who was the student and who was the instructor, seeing as

First solo in a Waco at Purdue University Airport in early Navy flight training, 1943

Roy as Corsair pilot in 1945

how everybody was just out of the service and all about the same age.

On the wall opposite the blackboard was a unique graph that took up nearly the entire length of the wall. The graph represented an entire private pilot's course, based on an average student's progress, hour by hour, maneuver by maneuver. This company, I thought, had a well-thought out program.

Just then Mrs. Hayden came out of her inner office with my papers and said to everyone present, "Boys, I'd like you to meet," and she turned my papers around and looked at them, "Our new instructor student, Roy Franklin."

I started to say, "Wrong name," but decided against it. The form had called for first name and middle initial.

Oh well, I thought, it won't matter much anyway, I'll probably be gone from here in a few weeks. Little did I know my future would be decided with and through these very people and that Virgie Hayden, the lady with my papers, had just spoken the name I would be known by for the rest of my life.

Later that evening I was still at the airport. Everybody had gone home except three fellows I had never met and myself. These three young men were busy putting the flight school's training planes away for the night. Being the new guy on the block I stood back and out of the way. The school's little trainers had no electrical systems so each of these men were taking turns starting the other fellow's engines by hand spinning their propellers. Once the engines were running, all three would taxi to a hangar which was on the other side of the airport, put their planes away and then walk back for three more. From the number of planes that were still parked on the flightline it looked to me like they had several trips yet.

It was getting late and beginning to get dark. I figured

if these guys were as hungry and as late for supper as I was, they probably would welcome some help. So… as the three walked up to the flight line once again, I said, "I'll help you," and climbed into the pilot's seat of one of the planes.

A guy about my size and age and wearing an Army Air Corps leather jacket with a set of silver wings, detached himself from the group and strode up to the nose of the plane.

"Switch off," he called.

"Switch off," I acknowledged.

He started pulling the propeller through, then stopped suddenly and peered intently at me through the windshield.

"Let's see now," he said, "Who are you? I mean, are you a student here?"

"Yes I am," I replied, with just a bit of sarcasm. Imagine a Navy pilot being grilled by an Army pilot!

He kept peering at me.

"I've never seen you here before, when did you start… I mean, how many lessons have you had?" he asked.

"Started today, one lesson," I answered.

"Well uh, don't you think you ought to have a couple more lessons before you taxi the plane by yourself?

I didn't know it at the time but this was Dean Fields, part owner and operator. Sensing something out of the ordinary by the amount of sputtering going on inside the plane, Dean suddenly asked, "What course are you taking?"

"Instructor," I growled.

"Contact," he shouted.

"Contact," I repeated, and off I taxied to the hangar.

Dean was a guy who loved a good story. Over the years he was able to stroke a number of hilarious versions out of that first meeting of ours, and he cracked up every time he told it.

Western Washington Aircraft was a well-run, friendly company. The first thing of note, as you stepped into their flight school's waiting room, was Virginia Hayden's smiling face. I swear that lady could cheer up the dreariest of moods! If you were there to take flight lessons or pay a bill, Virgie, as she was called, a pilot in her own right, was the person to take care of you. She and her husband, Bob, were partners in the flight school business along with the two Wilson boys, Dick and Chuck, and Dean Fields.

All the men partners were military-trained pilots. Bob, Dick and Chuck were all Navy-trained flyers, Dean an Army Air Corps-trained pilot.

Almost from the very beginning of military aviation there had been an ongoing rivalry between the Navy and the Air Corps. In this case Dean was outnumbered three to one but that didn't appear to faze him a bit. He was just the kind of guy who could handle about anything anybody wanted to throw at him, in fact, I think if anybody had been keeping score, they probably would have found Dean way ahead of the game.

For example, one day during coffee break there was a discussion concerning the various flying licenses held. It turned out that between the five of us, four of whom had been Navy pilots, only one had an honest to God seaplane rating and that was held by the one and only dry-land, bloody Air Corps pilot, Dean Fields! Oh how he cackled over that! Especially when Bob Hayden, during the War, had been a black-cat Catalina flying boat captain in the South Pacific. Regardless of his extensive saltwater experience, Bob did not have a civilian seaplane rating. Dean did! As the little session broke up, Dean called out, "If any of you Navy boys would like to learn to fly a seaplane, just let me know!" Cackle, cackle, cackle!

CHAPTER 3

Introduction to the San Juans
and Friday Harbor

Sometime in early 1947 I completed the instructor course and was hired by Western Washington Aviation for $200 bucks a month as a full-time flight instructor. One day, after three or four months of being an instructor, my flight school boss, Dick Wilson, called me into his office with an interesting proposal. One of my students, a guy from Orcas Island by the name of Bob Schoen, had started a scheduled flight service between the San Juan Islands and Bellingham. Schoen wanted to take some time off before he tackled his one pilot winter operation. Would I be willing to fly Schoen's schedules for a month while Schoen and his wife went on vacation?

Boy oh boy, would I! Schoen had been pretty sure I'd go for it so he was all set up to fly in tomorrow and give me an aircraft and an island route check.

I didn't get much sleep that night. Flying jobs in 1946 and 1947 were mighty hard to come by. In those days corporate flying, as we know it today, was virtually non-existent. The military? They were discharging, not hiring. The major airlines? They were swamped with applications from experienced, unemployed, multi-engined pilots.

The weather forecast for tomorrow was lousy. I had never flown in the Islands before nor had I ever ridden in a Stinson aircraft, much less fly one.

Sure, Schoen was a nice guy but we were talking about his brainchild, his airline. All night I thrashed the pillow. This was an opportunity I prayed to heaven I wouldn't screw up.

Sure enough, the next day proved the forecasters right. Pacing back and forth, I stopped for the umpteenth time by the window of the Flight Service office to gaze out at the windsock, the low drippy clouds scudding by, the murky restricted visibility. What a lousy day, I thought, to demonstrate what I didn't know about an airplane I'd never piloted before; in an unfamiliar area to boot.

Schoen's red Stinson Voyager whistled in overhead. A few moments later Bob taxied up, shut down his engine while still rolling, stepped out at what appeared to be the same instant the plane came to a stop—not hot-shot you understand, just complete mastery of the machine. Holy Mackerel, I thought, and I'm supposed to demonstrate to this guy my flying skills?

The way I figured it, I had two things going for me. Bob and I had always got along famously, and... I had been the flight instructor. Instructors are supposed to know a lot about...whatever? Maybe if I played it cool, I thought, maybe, just maybe I would be able to pull it off, I hoped.

This fellow, Bob Schoen, strongly built, perhaps five-ten, crewcut, maybe four or five years older than my 23 years, strode up, a big grin on his face.

"Hi, Roy," he said as he gave me a hearty handshake, "Ready to do some flying?" I acknowledged I was.

So... off we went.

The thing that saved the day was Bob himself. Bob has the type of personality, good-natured, friendly, no superior employer-employee attitude, a prince of a fellow who immediately puts a person at ease. Although we were buzzing along just above the treetops through wisps of mist and splatters of rain on the windshield, with Bob laughing and talking, I began to feel as though this beautiful little airplane, this country, this Bob Schoen and I were going to

Bob Schoen, my boss in 1947 at Orcas Island Air Service

get along just fine.

Flying out around the north end of Lummi Island, across the channel past Matia and Sucia Islands and coming up on Parker Reef, Bob said, "Start throttling her back, Roy, we are now on a left base for runway 16 at Orcas International."

"No kidding, where is this International runway?"

"Over there on the far side of that marsh—the little strip of gravel—see it?"

"Yeah—doesn't look like much."

"Hey man, that's the best strip in the County!"

I was too busy to comment.

As we touched down on the narrow strip of gravel, Bob said, "Stop her out here on the runway but keep the engine running." Oh, oh, I thought to myself, that's the kind of language I use when kicking a student flier out of the nest. I wondered just what my new boss had in mind. It didn't take long to find out.

Standing outside the plane, bracing the door against the blast of air from the propeller and shouting over the engine noise, Schoen conveyed the following message: "We are running about ten minutes late—you're due in Friday Harbor right now to pick up Mrs. Gallanger for Bellingham—good luck." With that he started to close the door.

"Hey, wait a minute," I shouted.

Disregarding instructions, I shut the engine off.

"Now Mr. Airline President, just where in hell is Friday Harbor?"

When Bob stopped laughing, he said, "fourteen miles, one hundred eighty degrees, second Island over--- you can't miss it."

"The airfield, what about the airfield? What does it look like? Where's it in relation to the town? How long is it? What kind of condition is it in? Is there a windsock?"

Schoen looked at his wristwatch, "Cow pasture, two miles west of town, we're late, you can't miss it, see you in a month"... and he was gone.

Bumbling along from one cloud-shrouded headland to another, trying this channel and that, I attempted to average somewhere close to Bob's quoted course of one hundred eighty degrees. It was not easy, the channels had directional ideas of their own; first one way and then another. As the time slipped by, those inevitable doubts began to assail me and a trickle of sweat began to drip off my nose. Darn it, I thought, if it wasn't for this low ceiling I could climb up to altitude and get my bearings.

Cranking around a bend in one of the channels, I suddenly came onto a pretty little seaport. It had to be the one I was looking for! Or was it? The International border, U.S. and Canada, was only three miles from where I had taken off on Orcas Island. Oh Lordy, I thought, if I have wandered off into the Canadian Islands, Mrs. Gallanger may have quite a wait, and Mrs. Franklin's husband will probably be looking for another job.

"Hey, good deal!" There on the roof of a waterfront building were the welcome words, "Friday Harbor," with an arrow pointing to the west. Ah, it was enough to put a song in one's heart!

Immediately I swung in over the village and rolled out on a westerly heading, humming a tune and thinking, this month's assignment is really going to be a breeze!

So I flew west. One hundred twenty miles an hour is two miles a minute, I told myself, so all I've got to do is fly one minute on this course and I'm there.

Strange... I have visually scoured every hayfield and cow pasture for the last three, coming on four miles and no runways, no parked planes, no windsock, no aircraft hangars? It seems inconceivable that a person could miss finding an airport which was only two miles from a town, but I certainly had. Reversing my course, known in the trade as doing a one-eighty, I flew back to Friday Harbor. Swinging out over the bay I came back in over town and lined up carefully on a west heading. Maybe I wasn't lined up exactly on course with that first run?

Again, studying every piece of grass big enough to land a plane on, I still could not spot anything that even remotely resembled an airfield. Time was slipping by. Angrily I reminded myself this flight was a scheduled passenger trip, not a Sunday afternoon sightseeing ride. But here I was, flubbing around, late, and couldn't even find the blankety-blank airport!

As the last resort, read the instructions, right? Or at least use the brain, as my school teacher mother would say. Maybe I was expecting too much? After all, Bob did say a cow pasture; and if that was really all it was, then where would Mrs. Gallanger be waiting…in the terminal? On a cow pasture? Not hardly---if she was still waiting at all for an airplane which was now 25 minutes late, she would be sitting in her car. A car? Had I seen a car out in a cow pasture somewhere? No, but I had just passed a pickup truck sitting on the edge of a chunk of grass big enough to land this plane in. I think.

Hauling the plane around in a steep bank, I swept in over the pickup truck. Doubts assailed me; maybe the truck had been parked there for a month? No, by George! Steam was coming out of the exhaust pipe. Somebody was running the engine! I'll land; if it isn't the right place at least they can tell me where the right place is.

What happened next is a perfect example of the old saying, "Haste makes waste."

Trying to hurry things up, I made the mistake of crowding in a bit too tight on my approach… ending up a shade high and a shade fast. You simply don't make that mistake on a small grass field and get away with it, especially when the grass is wet and slick from rain. I was about to find this out.

The truck I was interested in was parked alongside a small building, probably a sheep shed. No windsock, calm as far as I could tell, so I elected to land towards the truck; would save time if I could just roll right up to the door. Door to door service you might say.

Touching down at a good rate of speed, the truck and shed up ahead appeared to be growing in size very rapidly. I put on the brakes. Nothing happened. What the hell, no brakes? I shot a glance down at my left wheel; it wasn't turning! Too late! Not enough room left to make a belated go around! Brakes locked, wheel sliding almost unabated on the wet grass!

With a rush of hot blood to the face the realization dawned, I'm going to crack up this little airplane!

Desperate situations conjure up desperate thoughts; it flashed through my brain that nothing I had available or was doing was going to stop this skid except the crunching front end of that pickup truck. This throttle in my hand, connected to that engine out there, the combination of which had saved my butt from various situations more than once, was now on the wrong end of this machine to do me any good. The instant that thought seared across my brain I immediately threw all efforts into forcing the plane to turn end-for-end.

Releasing the right brake and jamming in the left rudder and brake, I prayed for a groundloop. Normally, a swerving, out-of-control, wing-dragging, tire screeching, ground rotation called a groundloop is just about one of the most embarrassing things that can happen to a pilot; in this case I was praying for one!

However…wet, rain-slick grass is not the same as dry concrete. With the left brake and rudder pedal just about shoved through the floor, only a slight deviation in direction was discernable.

I'm staring right into the front of that pickup truck and into the face of disaster!

Really not sure what happened next? Whether I hit a little patch of gravel or what; all I know is the brake suddenly grabbed, the plane swapped ends and we were now sliding backwards just about as fast as we had been sliding forwards.

I shoved the throttle wide open.

The reaction was amazing. The instant the engine came up to full power, trying its best to drag the airplane in the opposite direction, it felt to me like a huge parachute had just opened!

The plane came to a stop almost immediately---right in front of the shed and about one plane length from the pickup.

With palsied hand I pulled the throttle back to idle, shut the engine off, pried my feet from the brake pedals and got out of the plane---very slowly—on very spongy legs. Carefully I reached out and got a grip on the wing strut; wouldn't want to fall on one's face in front of one's passengers, now would we?

Sure enough, there were people in the pickup, a man and a woman. They didn't move. Believe me I was feeling about as low as a person can get. After the inept demonstration these people had just witnessed, I really couldn't imagine anybody wanting to fly with me. The fact nobody was getting out of the truck pretty much confirmed my worst fears. Just as I was considering suicide a cheerful young woman climbed out of the truck and paddled up to me in her galoshes.

"This is Bob Schoen's airplane?", she asked. I lamely admitted it was.

She confirmed that her name was Gallanger.

I stood waiting for the axe.

The next words this lovely lady said will be etched in my memory forever.

She said, "Well let's go! I told my husband I would ride anywhere with a pilot who could handle a plane like you just did!"

As we flew along on our course to Bellingham, Mrs. Gallanger and me, I silently made a vow to myself; to diligently work to become the skilled pilot this cheerful and trusting lady thought I was.

In the thousands and thousands of flights I flew in the next 32 years, winter and summer, day and night, I never injured a passenger. I believe I kept my vow.

CHAPTER 4

A Student With Airplane Fever

Bob Schoen's original flight schedules were designed for the convenience of the Island residents. The daily flights consisted of a morning roundtrip and an afternoon roundtrip between the Islands and the mainland city of Bellingham, all flights beginning and ending in the Islands. Since my residence during this one month assignment was still on the mainland, it meant I had to deadhead out to the Islands each morning to start the morning's scheduled departure. It was the reverse in the evening; fly the final schedule of the day to the Islands and then deadhead back home.

In view of the flying company's profit and loss sheet, and the spotty traffic of those days, my wages and the extra trips on the plane undoubtedly added to the mass of red ink. But what the heck, let the boss worry about that, I was having the time of my life! Sure, it was a seven day a week commitment, but the weather was good, traffic was light, I had a brand new airplane to fly... and someone else was paying the bills!

To top it all off, I was the envy of every flight instructor and student on the Bellingham airport! Many a long, hungry look followed me as I rolled by... my six cylinder, 150 hp Franklin air-cooled engine purring like a kitten, the Stinson name and its emblem, a drawn bow painted on my tail; a big, lovely scroll down each side of the fuselage, reading, "Orcas Island Air Service," WOW!

Several times in late afternoon while driving the

"Limo" from downtown Bellingham to the airport for the final day's flight to the Islands, I picked up a tall, slim fellow about my age, who was hitchhiking.

I knew him; his name was Al Kiel. He was an infantry veteran and he was married to a former next door neighbor of mine, Jean Hitt. Al had a job at the Bellingham Furniture Factory; didn't own a car and under his present financial situation, he said, couldn't afford one. So every day he was hitchhiking. That was a pretty tough assignment. To make sure he was to work on time, it meant leaving home every morning real early, rain or shine. Then walking and thumbing rides all the way home after a long day of labor.

I admired his determination, but of course that didn't help him very much since the airport entrance was all the further I could take him, and that was usually only two or three miles from where I'd picked him up. About the third time this happened I had an idea.

"Al," I said, "Why don't you go on this flight with me? I'm just going to run this passenger out to Orcas Island and then I'm coming right back; would be happy to have your company."

Al didn't answer immediately but I could see he was working on it. I knew he had never flown before. I also knew his wife had some definite opinions as to married men, especially fathers, flying airplanes.

"When you get back, are you going right home?" Al asked.

"Sure am," I answered, "Go right past your house. I'll drop you off."

"Jean is going to kill me when she finds out," Al muttered, "But I'm going to do it! Yes siree, I'm going to do it!"

It usually doesn't take long to determine whether a person is going to like flying. With Al there was no question—

he was all over the plane, peering out this window and then that one, pointing out places he recognized, chuckling in amazement as a miniature panorama unfolded beneath our wings.

On the trip back, I let him take a try at the controls. Like all of us on our first try, he was all over the sky—one wing low, skidding, slipping, yo-yoing up and down!

After that, if Al wasn't waiting alongside the highway for me, he would be standing at the airport entrance, and if he wasn't there, he would have caught a ride direct to the airport.

Of course, there wasn't always room on the outbound flight for Al. The first couple of times that happened I knew he was pretty disappointed. But then I began to notice a change.

"It's okay," he would say, "I don't mind waiting. I'll just wander around and look at the airplanes and talk to some of the pilots."

One afternoon when I picked him up on the highway I began to be suspicious. The main thing was, he showed practically no enthusiasm when I told him I had no passengers booked for the flight; that with only outbound freight, he would be able to fly the plane both ways! Normally that would have put him on cloud nine; instead he avoided my eyes and did a lot of looking out the window.

"What's the matter, Al?" I asked, "The wife put two and two together and figure out why you are always riding home with me?"

"No," he answered.

"Are you going to fly with me on this flight?"

"No, I can't."

"Why not?"

Al turned in his seat and looked me right in the eye, "Because," he said with a sudden twinkle in his eyes, "I'm scheduled for my second flight lesson."

So that's what he's been doing while waiting for his ride home! Signing up for a GI flight training course!

"You old son-of-a-gun!" I exclaimed, "When did you take your first dual flight?"

"Yesterday, while I was waiting for you," he answered.

"Your wife know about this?"

"Not yet."

"When are you going to tell her?"

Al squirmed and said he was still looking for the right moment. I didn't say anything further. I could see this had all the makings of a future situation.

Each evening, by the time I was back from the Islands and had serviced my plane and tied it down, Al was through with his lesson. Shortly thereafter, we would be on our way home.

This handy little arrangement was only about a week old when things hit the fan. I had just turned into Al's driveway to drop him off when a determined looking Mrs. Kiel suddenly appeared by my side of the car. She motioned me to roll down my window. Cautiously I rolled it down an inch or so. She motioned for more. Not wanting to look guilty or anything, I complied; after all, Jean and I had been raised on adjoining farms and had known each other all of our lives.

Jean leaned partly in my window and very calmly said, "You have been dropping my husband off here in our driveway for a week now and you haven't once come in to say hello, why?"

Looking me right in the eye, she let me stutter over excuses like, "It was always so late," and... "I had to get home." That's when she dropped the meg-a-tonner, "It wouldn't have anything to do with my husband taking flying lessons would it?"

From the passenger's side of the car I heard a long sigh, like from a little kid who hadn't made it to the bathroom in time.

"Flying lessons?" I croaked.

Mrs. Kiel ignored me.

"Boys," she said, "I'm in no mood for games. For the last week, whenever my dear husband doesn't think I'm watching, he's over there doing maneuvers with his hands. Don't forget, Roy, I was raised next door to you; I know a case of airplane fever when I see it. Besides... I found a flight manual on the floor under the bed." A very uncomfortable silence descended, followed by a terse statement that had all the earmarks of an order, "I want to see both of you guys in the house." What that, she turned and stalked into the house. Al and I exchanged a long look. Without a word spoken, we meekly followed.

Very quietly the two of us entered the kitchen. Jean was pouring three cups of coffee. She only said one word, "Sit." We sat. Putting the pot back on the stove, Jean came and sat down. No one spoke. All was quiet except for a baby fussing in the next room. Jean got up and in a moment came back carrying an infant in her arms.

It has been said, "An angry woman can be a formidable adversary; an angry woman with a child in her arms can be pure hell on wheels." Things didn't look good, that's for sure!

Jean spoke. "I'm angry, really angry, and I think I've got every right to be. Both of you guys knew right from the beginning how I felt about a husband of mine flying, but you went right ahead and did it anyway. The fact that I've changed my mind about Al's flying is neither here nor there. What really gripes me is that neither one of you guys had the guts to come and talk to me about it."

Al sat transfixed, staring at his wife, his coffee cup suspended in midair. Slowly he set his cup down and stood up. He might have been a seasoned combat veteran but from the look on his face I would say he was about to burst into tears.

Jumping up, I kissed Jean on the cheek and ran for my car.

Al proved to be a keen and dedicated student. Over the next year or so he completed his flying course and received his license, all the time working hard and supporting his growing family. The last I heard, Al and Jean were living in Renton, Washington, had four children and were doing well. Al, I understood, had gone into electronics and was the foreman of a shift at Boeing Aircraft Company's missile division.

CHAPTER 5

The Whippet

Dean Fields took special interest in Bob Schoen's commuter airline experiment, especially now that his employee, me, was involved. Almost every time I was loading or unloading the plane or car at Bellingham Airport, sure enough, there would be good old Dean, watching. Dean's coffee break stories were hilarious, especially if they involved Orcas Island Air Service's downtown limo. He loved that one! I better fill you in...

The Orcas Island Air Service airport limousine that was used in 1947 to carry passengers between Bellingham's airport and downtown Bellingham was one of Bob Schoen's greatest pride and joys. It was a 1926 Whippet two-door touring car. The Whippet was painted black and the name 'Orcas Island Air Service' was emblazoned on each side in big bold white letters. The Whippet had the old fashioned two-wheeled brake system, an ooga, ooga horn and a battery under the bench-type front seat that was constantly shorting out from a bad terminal connection. With no backup limo and a time schedule that kept a person hopping every minute that you were on the ground in Bellingham, the corroded battery connection was just something the Whippet pilot-driver had to put up with.

Flying a typical scheduled flight into Bellingham from the Islands, the pilot on landing at the airport would unload his passengers and freight from the plane and reload them into the Whippet. He would then head into town, providing, of course, the Whippet would start. If it wouldn't, no big deal, just jerk out the front seat, climb in and stomp with your heel on the battery terminal a couple of times. This usually took care of the problem, and away she would go.

One of the advantages of leaving the passengers waiting by the plane while you walked over to the parking lot to get the Whippet, was... you could go through this battery stomping routine in private without having to answer a lot of embarrassing questions, like, "Why don't you have the damn thing fixed?" Once old Betsy was running, you didn't ever want to make the mistake of shutting her off until you were through with her. If you did, chances were you would have to go through the battery routine all over again.

Fixing the problem would of course have been the thing to do--- but the trouble wasn't just a loose connection; both the battery cable and the battery itself needed replacing. Times were tough, business was spotty, we were trying to conserve—so every day or so, when the stomping wouldn't quite do it, I would wedge a couple of nails into the trouble spot. This would usually be enough to satisfy a temporary electrical connection.

I hasten to add while we may have jury-rigged a car now and then, no corners were ever cut when it came to our aircraft maintenance. Twenty years of accident-free flying attests to that.

So now we have a sizzling hot day. The streets and sidewalks of downtown Bellingham are filled with people. I'm hot and frazzled. The Whippet and I have been fighting traffic to deliver people here and there, pick up outgoing freight—all the time pressing to be at the Leopold Hotel by our advertised passenger pickup time.

Finally... the old Whippet and I leave the front of the hotel with a load of innocent and unsuspecting air travelers for Orcas Island, Waldron Island and points west. We drive the half block to Bellingham's main intersection, Cornwall and Holly, and stop for the light. A steady stream of people crowd by on the crosswalk; cars shoot by. The light changes; we make a convulsive leap into the intersection and the engine dies!

That blankety-blank battery!

With two people occupying the front bench-seat with me, I've got to ask them to climb out into the honking and rushing traffic while I jerk up the seat and stomp on the battery connection. Although I'm focusing total concentration on the moves required, nevertheless I am aware of the confusion around us and also of a strange keening sound in the air, like an Indian woman wailing for her dead.

1926 Whippet and 1947 Stinson Voyager at Orcas Island

Slamming the seat back in place, I leap in and give the engine a try; it works!

I leap out and as I'm helping my passengers back into the car I look around for the source of this strange keening sound.

Oh no! It's that bloody Army Air Corps pilot, Dean Fields, the one with the seaplane rating! He is leaning against a lamp post, holding his sides and literally howling! People have gathered around him and are laughing and pointing at us. Being exasperated enough, as it was, this merriment of Dean's did not help my frame of mind one bit; in fact it had a direct bearing on what happened next.

As I squeezed the Whippet past the policeman who was attempting to unsnarl traffic, I stuck my tongue out at the Army pilot. In that instant of distraction my line of traffic stopped. Fortunately there was no damage done, just a loud bang when the Whippet nuzzled the next car's rear end. This unfortunate collision occurred while Dean Fields and I were having momentary eye contact and it seemed to have a devastating effect on him, as he now started sliding down the lamp pole as though he was about to collapse!

But I knew what that yo-yo was doing; he was laughing his tonsils out! With a sinking heart I knew just as sure as anything that I was going to hear about this little episode until time immortal.

That's life I guess.

I went out and bought a new battery and cable and charged it to the boss.

CHAPTER 6

Back to the Flight School

Bob Schoen was back and on the job. My month's assignment was over and it was time to go back to the flight school. I would never be the same.

The San Juan Islands had proven to be one of the most magnificent areas I had ever seen. The people... farmers, fishermen, loggers, mechanics, carpenters, shop owners and wives and kids, they were my kind of people. They made me feel right at home. Somehow, someday, I would live there. But for now, that dream would have to wait.

Reluctantly, I went back to the flight school.

Actually, it was kind of fun getting back to the old group; like going back to school after the summer vacation. As we saw in an earlier chapter, Dean Fields could make any day fun. Fortunately for the rest of us, there was one person connected to the flight school, who, as it turned out, could match Dean Field's wit and humor. This person was a local Bellingham veterinarian and flyer by the last name of McKenzie. I don't know what his first name was; everybody just called him Doc. I understood Doc had taken some of the flight school's courses, although that was before my time; maybe even learned to fly there?

Anyway, this veterinarian was an adventurous and lovable character and he flew a beautiful, brand-new, fire engine red, four-place Bellanca CruiseMaster. Everyone associated with the flight school thought the world of Doc and of his airplane; in that order I'm sure. Doc's

CruiseMaster was the fastest and the most aerodynamically efficient civilian airplane in the area (180 mph with only a 190 hp engine!).

In these early post-war days, United Airlines was running a schedule into Bellingham from Seattle with a DC-3. Doc loved to let the United flight depart Bellingham ahead of him and then take off in his relatively tiny, red Bellanca and pass them up! That really made those United pilots sit up and take notice!

Doc and Dean were kindred souls, liked each other and were constantly and good naturedly sparring—verbally, that is.

Somewhere along the line, Dean found out the date of Doc's birthday, so he wrapped up a present, addressed it to Doc and left it at the office.

Doc was really touched. He found it hard to believe Dean knew of his birthday, much less would go to the trouble of giving him a present.

Doc eagerly unwrapped the package.

There for all to see was one old and tattered GI handkerchief! Neatly laundered and folded, but worn and tattered.

Doc was very gracious in accepting this gift. The fact he was able to keep his face straight amidst all the chuckles was cause for much speculation (and anticipation) of what the inevitable retaliation would be.

Christmas 1947 was rapidly approaching. A pretty little decorated Christmas tree stood in the corner of Virgie's flight office. One day a gaily wrapped package appeared under this tree. It was a good-sized package and it was addressed to Dean Fields... and it was from Doc McKenzie!

Wow! Talk about imaginations running wild!

With Doc being a veterinarian and all, some of the

speculation on what might be inside that package got pretty creative, to say the least.

Finally the day arrived and all personnel assembled for the company Christmas party.

Everyone crowded around as Dean unwrapped his gift. It was a toilet seat sawn in half and lined with fur. The caption read:

MERRY CHRISTMAS
A FUR LINED THUNDERMUG
FOR A HALF ASSED PILOT

EEGADS! The Army Air Corps pilot (with the seaplane rating) had just met his match!

CHAPTER 7

To Friday Harbor With a Second Stinson

Sometime after Christmas, Bob Schoen contacted me at the flight school with some electrifying news. He had purchased a second Stinson Voyager. In the Spring he intended to base this new plane at Friday Harbor, the seat of San Juan County. He would need a pilot; would I be interested in the job?

"Would I be interested in the job?... Holy Mackerel Schoen, you just hired yourself a pilot!"

No, I wasn't excited at all... not the slightest bit... I just could hardly sleep for the rest of the winter without waking up with a grin on my face!

The neat thing about the offer... it wasn't just another one of those GI dreams of, "Come Spring, I might do this or that." Nope, this fellow, Schoen, already had the second plane purchased and he had just hired "Yours Truly" to fly it. The next moves were up to me.

Following the Christmas and New Years' holidays, I called a real estate company that was listed in the Island phone book. They said they would meet me at King's field on whatever day and time I specified. Great! With my new future boss's blessing, my Mother and I took off in the new Stinson for Friday Harbor. Wife Margaret Ann was not able to accompany us; she had just given birth to our first child, Steve.

The weather was beautiful as my Mother and I flew over San Juan County's enchanted islands. Mom pointed out Rosario, Robert Moran's beautiful home and estate on Orcas Island, and told me about when she was a girl and living on Orcas and how much she loved to sit and listen to Mr. Moran play his pipe organ (which was two stories high!).

Circling the little seaport of Friday Harbor, I said, "Well Mom, there is my new home."

"From up here, it looks like a lovely place; hope there is a house available for you," commented practical Mom.

Buzzing the sheep off the grass landing strip, we landed and parked the plane. A man who had been standing there by his car came over and introduced himself as Bill Suttles from Geoghegan Realty.

On the way into town the realtor informed us that houses on the Island were in short supply. "As you probably know," he said, "Friday Harbor is not very big and with our returning veterans making up for lost time, there just isn't much housing left. In fact, he said, "the only thing he had at the moment were two houses that "might" be for sale, plus there was a 40 acre piece of land for sale. He had no rentals at all. The forty acre piece has no buildings, just a house foundation... but the foundation is brand new!" he quickly added.

"A foundation but no house, what's that all about," I asked. One of those unfortunate things," he said, "a veteran's dreams that were bigger than his pocket book. He poured the foundation and then left the Island, taking his house plans with him. The bank repossessed the property but so far nobody has come up with a house plan that fits the foundation!

I explained to the realtor again, that what I was looking for was a rental unit. "Well," he said, "I don't know, all we can do is talk to these people. They have mentioned sale but nothing has been said about rental."

The two possible houses were both in town; one, a very small, single story, 400 square foot house, the other, a big two-story house. By the time afternoon rolled around the owners of both of these houses had definitely made up their minds to sell. Neither house owner was willing to go into the rental business.

This put me into a bind. Like most veterans I didn't have the means to finance a steak dinner, much less purchase a home. Besides, basing one's future on a light plane flying job in 1948 was pretty risky. The only thing I really had going for me was the good feeling I had about this Bob Schoen and his fascinating dream of establishing a scheduled island airline. I soon found myself accompanying the realtor to the local bank to explore the possibilities of a loan.

The San Juan County Bank president, Cecil Carter, just about flipped his wig when he found out I flew for a living. It seems the last flying outfit on the Island had departed owing considerable money.

Fortunately for all us vets, Uncle Sam, with his GI bill, was co-signing mortgage notes for us. The bank's vice-president, Bob Gregory, quietly confirmed this. When I left the bank it was with the assurance the bank would finance a home purchase of mine, up to $7,000. That was a lot of money in those days.

Armed with the bank's blessings, Mom and I took another look at the two houses. I had no inkling of it at the time (found out about it several years later) but our inspection of the two-story house caused a bit of a panic. The thing was, nobody knew who we were. To my request to see the basement, the lady of the house said, "Help yourself," which I did. About the time I had taken two steps down, she remembered with a terrible shock, her husband and his buddy, Dutch, had hung last night's poached deer down there.

Sure, I noticed a dressed carcass hanging in the basement… but with no hide, head or feet on it, I assumed it was a domestic animal. I understand the instant the realtor and his customers left the premises a mad scramble was made to dispose of the evidence. It caused a big laugh some years later.

Thinking only in terms of my then small family, I decided the two-story house was way too big. Lack of foresight? How was I to know what a few years of salt air and island living would do for the wife and me? The contract read, $3,200 at four percent interest, no down payment required, thirty dollars per month and the little house was all ours!

Just before dark, feeling like we had put in a pretty good day's work, my Mother and I prepared for takeoff. During the 'run-up' my propeller caused quite a halo of vapor. Noticing it, Mom said, "I've never seen that before, what is it?"

"I'm thinking maybe we should have left earlier," I answered, "when a propeller does that it means the air is getting close to total saturation. Around here that means fog; we better be getting a move on!"

When we reached our cruising altitude the sight that greeted my eyes was not very encouraging. The whole area clear to the Cascade Mountains on the mainland seemed completely covered by a blanket of fog! Judging by the amount of murky haze in the atmosphere below us, it wouldn't be long before the Islands would be going under also.

"How beautiful!" my mother exclaimed, "Like cotton candy!" "Yes Mom, cotton candy full of rock candy."

The instant my vacuum tube radio warmed up I knew there were some unusual things happening. Bellingham Radio was talking to a Trans World Airways flight.

Bellingham was also giving an Alaskan Airlines flight an airport landing advisory. Those major carriers never came into Bellingham… what was going on?

As soon as I could get a word in edgewise I established contact with Bellingham Radio. The radio operator, Fred Cook, came back with, "How far out are you, Roy?"

"Ten, maybe twelve minutes, why?"

"You'll never make it, Roy, a fog bank is rolling in right now; we will be under in less than five minutes. Seattle, Portland, everything," he added, "is down; how's it out there?"

"Shutting down fast, Fred, but we will be all right, we're changing course for Orcas Island right now. As we hurried up Orcas Island's Eastsound I stayed tuned to the Bellingham frequency. It seemed to be only a minute or so after the Alaskan flight reported on the ground that Bellingham airport reported going zero-zero.

It was a close shave… we just did get on the ground at Orcas before the fog rolled in. Bob Schoen came out to the airport and picked my Mother and me up. We were the Schoen's 'drop-in' guests for the next several nights.

Listening to the broadcast radio that evening we learned that the entire West Coast was fogged in. Bellingham, the most northerly airfield on the U.S. West Coast had been the last to go under. Air traffic inbound to Seattle from Alaska and the Pacific area had changed course for Bellingham. Everybody was safely on the ground. Fog sat down so tight on the highways that Greyhound buses, dispatched from Seattle to the Bellingham airport to pick up the stranded passengers, had to slow down to a crawl and were late arriving.

According to the news, there were more four-engined airplanes parked on Bellingham's airport than had ever been seen there before. The little airport restaurant had been suddenly and unexpectedly inundated with hundreds of people; food had run out; there was looting and burning- -- No! No! I just threw that in for the heck of it. No looting and burning in those days, just some disappointed, hungry people.

On the second day of fog, at one o'clock in the afternoon, the ceiling at Bellingham raised for about 30 minutes—up to 200 feet and the visibility stretched to one mile; then it shut down again. None of the big airliners moved; there was nowhere to go.

Having observed Bellingham's mid-day trend, Mom and I were loaded and ready to go by noon on the following day. Orcas Airport is at sea level. Bellingham Airport has an elevation of 158 feet. The distance between the two airfields is 17 miles. When Bellingham reported their ceiling had risen to 100 feet and their visibility was up to one mile, we launched. We had a definite ceiling and our visibility was adequate. If we couldn't get through, we would climb. Our ace in the hole was Yakima, on the other side of the Cascade Mountains. No coastal fog over there... Yakima was less than two hours away and we had four hours of fuel onboard.

This was an interesting flight. Flocks of ducks wintering over in the salt water, flushing up ahead of our low flying plane, then peeling off to left and right when overtaken. A pod of Orca blowing their steamy breath into the chilly air; a tugboat plowing along, pulling a huge bargeload of wood chips, undoubtedly destined for one of the mainland paper mills.

Crossing the shipping channel, we pivoted around Lummi Island's Point Megly, then proceeded down Hales Pass between Lummi Island and the Lummi Indian Reservation on the mainland. Fog hanging in the trees both left and right; adequate clearance over the water. Half way down Hales Pass the woods on our left side suddenly dropped away with only a beach showing... the portage! Banking across the waterway we rolled out on our new course, crossing the portage with wings level and ready to climb if necessary. It wasn't necessary; the railroad overpass on Marine drive was dead ahead. Beyond the overpass I knew was a long grass field that led to Bellingham's abandoned northeast southwest runway...plenty good for an Island airplane!

Taxiing in, I could hardly believe the number of airliners parked everywhere! They towered over us, huge and silent, wreathed in delicate streamers of vapor. It was like watching an Alfred Hitchcock movie---beautiful but spooky!

The Bellingham newspaper said the Orcas Island Air Service airplane was the only aircraft to land at the Bellingham Airport during the record five-day fog.

Wife, Margaret Ann, was sure happy about the new house, our first, although she would have to wait almost two months before we could make the move to Friday Harbor. It was a long two months of waiting for both of us.

CHAPTER 8

Moving to Friday Harbor With Island Sky Ferries

Sometime during that winter or early spring, Schoen changed the company name from Orcas Island Air Service to Island Sky Ferries Inc. The Company would retain that new name for the next 21 years and through three different ownerships. Another earthshaking change—the 1926 Whippet was gone and a modern four-door 1941 DeSoto had taken its place.

Employment for me was to start April 1, 1948 in Friday Harbor. On the 10th of March, with the 1936 Ford towing our possessions in my Dad's two-wheeled trailer, the family and I departed for the seaport of Anacortes. There we boarded a Black Ball ferry for the San Juan Archipelago. Margaret Ann was 19, Steve was three months, and I was 23.

This voyage on the ferry provided Margaret Ann with her first view of the San Juan Islands, my second by boat, Steve's first everything. Walking the exposed deck with our son, the wind blowing our hair, we pointed out the sights to the boy; the seals in the water, the screaming gulls, the little fishing boats, the whitecaps, the roll of the boat. Just before he yawned and dropped off to sleep a little smile flickered across his lips. I turned to his Mother and said, "See that! This kid is going to be an Islander!"

As we rounded yet another bend in one of the many channels, suddenly there it was! Our new home! The little village port of Friday Harbor!

Not many people coming and going in those days. As we drove off the ferry and up Friday Harbor's main street, the few people on the sidewalks stopped and stared. Margaret Ann turned to me with a concerned look on her face and said, "They don't look any too friendly." I laughed, "Probably wondering if I'm the new game warden." I had no idea until years later of just how accurate that offhand remark had been.

Ah, our first home, all 520 square feet of it! Guard Street in front, an alley behind, a church on one side and Sam and Effie Bridge's home on the other. In front of our house and across Guard Street was an orchard and a two-story house, soon to be replaced by a new high school and gymnasium.

This little house of ours was approximately 22 feet square... plus a lean-to that housed a bathroom and laundry area. The house interior was divided into four equal rooms; two bedrooms, a living room and a dining-room/kitchen. The house was heated by a Spark oil heater in the living room and an oil-fired cook stove in the kitchen. The kitchen stove not only cooked our meals but also furnished us, through copper coils in the firebox, with a hot water supply. The house had high ceilings, no insulation and a tall, distorted single-pane window in each room. No refrigerator or dishwasher. On a wall of the kitchen was mounted one of those huge old-fashioned crank-telephones. I suppose nowadays a person would have to go to a museum to see a telephone like that. On the back of the lot was an open car garage and several big fir trees... and between the garage and the house was an area for our vegetable garden.

About the same time as Bob Schoen was expanding his Air Service by basing an airplane and pilot in Friday Harbor, a Bellingham seaplane company was doing the same thing. This seaplane company had been flying charter with a two/three place Cessna. Now their new Friday Harbor division consisted of one young, single, former Army Air Corps pilot named Bill Savage and a Cessna 140 seaplane. Savage bunked in the pigeon loft of Brown Lumber Company's building, which at that time was on the Friday Harbor waterfront.

By the time the second division arrived, (that was Savage and me), the Island inhabitants were not sure if we were here to stay or would we fade out like an earlier post-war aviation operation had done. It took awhile for the locals to take us seriously. However, since water and boats were their norm and all the seaplane activity was in full view of town, citizens took to Bill Savage's seaplane service more quickly than they did to the Bob Schoen/Roy Franklin cow pasture operation.

An interesting happening—the seaplane company's island business, under Savage's local tutelage, was doing very well. The owner of the seaplane company was elated and soon decided to expand by taking on a new pilot/partner who had some bucks to invest. Unfortunately for the seaplane company, the owner and his new partner decided they would no longer need Savage. The thing they overlooked was... Islanders don't care who owns the airplane, it's the pilot they trust and ride with. Savage had that figured out. He went out and bought a seaplane of his own and everyone lived happily ever after...except the Bellingham seaplane outfit... their Island traffic disappeared like a morning mist.

So it was Savage with his Marine Air and me with Schoen's Island Sky Ferries competing for the favors of the few locals who wished to fly. When the wind was howling, however, or the foghorns were groaning, Bill Savage and I would happily pick up our rifles and go hunting together. During those early, lean years, it was rabbits year around and pheasants, ducks and deer in season… all-important additions to both of our family tables.

One day Bert King was flying with me from Bellingham to his Friday Harbor home. Bert was telling me of the good meat-market purchase he had made in Bellingham, 39 cents a pound for turkey. I said, "For heaven sakes Bert, why would you buy turkey when you have hundreds of rabbits running around loose on your farm?" He looked at me and said, "We don't eat them." That night I was telling my wife about Bert's rabbit statement, "We don't eat them." She and I just couldn't understand why Bert would say something like that. To us the rabbits tasted almost like chicken… and they were free!

Those first years after the war were tough. We ate a lot of rabbit. Eventually it happened… I walked into our kitchen when my wife, Margaret Ann, was frying some rabbit for dinner. I stopped… I couldn't take another step… I said, "Honey, I hate to say this but I don't think I can ever eat another rabbit." She gave me a long steady look, picked up the skillet, saying, "Me too," and handed it all to me. I carried dinner outside for the dog.

The dog came up, took one sniff and walked away.

Ah yes, when I told Bert about what happened, he said, "When I grew up I swore I'd never eat another rabbit."

As with any new endeavor such as this daily scheduled flying service, in and out of unimproved cow pastures with marginally powered single-engined airplanes, there were many, many things we had to learn… more times than not, the hard way. For example, during turbulent air conditions there was a heavy clunking being transmitted throughout my assigned aircraft. Already having a question concerning these little cloth-covered wings, this mysterious "CLUNK" really had me concerned. Like a guy once said, "Only my laundress knows how much it bothers me."

On the ground I wrenched and pulled on the wings and struts, rocking the plane violently up and down... but to no avail. The boss and I talked about it and we tried, but we could not duplicate that CLUNK.

One day during a nasty 'southeaster,' the boss was sitting in his car directly under my landing approach. I was getting banged around pretty good and that CLUNK was really pronounced! Schoen drove up to where I was unloading and as soon as our customers were out of earshot, he said, "Something is wrong with your landing gear, it was flopping around in that rough air like it was broken."

The Stinson landing gear is tremendously strong but the rough fields had really done a job on the shock absorbers. The seals in the oleo struts were worn out; the hydraulic fluid had thus been pumped out, leaving the oleos dry and the gear flopping. From then on our landing gears got special scrutiny and service and my mysterious CLUNK disappeared.

Another learning experience came within a hair's breath of disaster. We were still flying with wooden propellers. Metal ones were expensive and probably unnecessary. On this particular day I was flying the morning schedule from Bellingham to the Islands. I had landed at Orcas, dropped off some freight and was now, with Elmer Severson on board, departing Orcas for Waldron Island. Just as we lifted off the ground at Orcas a pheasant rooster flushed up out of the grass and into our propeller. It hit on my side with a solid impact; blood, guts and feathers! It was the first time I had hit that large a bird. I quickly swung around and landed. The impact had been considerable. Elmer and I really looked that propeller over carefully. Except for some blood staining, there appeared to be no damage to the propeller.

After dropping Elmer off, I departed Waldron for Friday Harbor. While approaching the west end of Shaw

Island at 800 feet, a sudden violent shaking hit the front end of the airplane. Smoke boiled out of the engine area and part of the engine cowl came loose and flew back against the windshield. The shaking was so violent that my vision was blurred. It was as though the whole engine had blown up! I immediately shut off the engine. When the propeller stopped turning the shaking stopped and there sticking up in the air, looking at me, was the jagged, broken end of the propeller.

Yellow Island and Crane Island were the only terra firma reachable. No beaches, no farm fields, all were woods and water; it would have to be a water ditching. This lovely new airplane was probably flying its last flight. The narrow pass between Crane Island and Orcas Island, called Pole Pass, looked the best. There I would have a better chance of swimming to Orcas's inhabited shore... and perhaps later I would have a chance to salvage the plane. Thank God I had no passengers on board.

A 10 or 12 knot southwesterly wind was blowing. I had immediately turned and was now gliding downwind... losing altitude rapidly. It was obvious it was going to take all of my altitude just to reach the pass. I would have no altitude left or room to turn back into the wind. That was not good. I had no illusions as to the outcome. With no shoulder harness or helmet, with a non-retractable landing gear and traveling downwind fast... the plane would hit hard, flip onto its back and sink. Me too, if I was knocked unconscious.

No radio, no boats visible.

Now I am entering the narrow gut of the pass... big fir trees on either side... Crane on the left, Orcas on the right. A flash view of a house and small clearing on Crane—instinctively I turn towards it. Instantly, but too late to rectify, I realize I have made a potentially fatal error...

I have trapped myself in the notch of a little cove. With no power and no room, there is no way out. To keep from ramming the cove's sidewall I'm momentarily in a wild vertical bank to the left and sinking with the wind as it spills over the island. In my face, like a massive picket fence, a line of tall fir trees stands between me and the clearing. I'm below their level... I can't make it! BAM! I hit the trees.

There would be many times in the future when I would ponder over those next few seconds. Could it be possible the good Lord figured I was worth saving? After all, He knew if He interceded now and then, He could get 30 years worth of flying midnight medical cases out of me. Something like that must have happened because what happened next had nothing to do with pilot skill.

The plane in a vertical bank slammed through the solid crosshatch of limbs without touching the trunks of the trees. Covered with limbs and out of flying speed the plane stalled and rolled to the right in what they used to call an over-the-top-stall, unbelievably hitting the steep upsloping ground squarely on both main wheels. The impact would have collapsed most landing gears. Although the Stinson's tires were mashed flat, jamming dirt and grass between the tires and the wheels, the gear held. The plane made a spine-snapping bounce, the rising ground coming up to catch it. Instinctively I jammed on the brakes. The plane and I slid up to and stopped within four meet of a fenced garden by the side of a small cottage.

Slowly I became aware of being still alive... and at about the same time I became aware of a woman just ten feet from the nose of the airplane. Her back was turned and she was bending over thinning carrots. With the combination of her bad hearing, no engine noise and the wind blowing, she was completely unaware of my presence.

Ever since the realization had seared into my mind

that I had made a fatal mistake by turning my powerless plane into this dead end cove, I had been functioning in what might be described as a numbed, robot-like state. When I crawled out of the airplane my legs would not hold me. I was glad the lady still had not seen me. Frankly, it took several tries before I could even speak.

When she did hear my unexpected voice so close to her, it really gave her a start. Nothing, however, compared to her speechless, open-mouthed reaction when she turned and looked into the front end of an airplane! I don't know which of us, she or I, was in the worse shape. Like me, it took her awhile to find her voice. "Whaa...Who are... How...?"

"M-m-m-am, I--I need to use your t-t-telephone."

Probably if things had been more normal this lady might have said, "Sonny, what you need is a bathroom." Anyway, I finally got through to her and she, in turn, made me to understand the closest telephone was on the other side of the Pass, on Orcas. Never taking her eyes off my airplane, she slowly mumbled, "You can use the rowboat."

So I took the rowboat. By phone I got hold of Rich Exton, a friend and Orcas Island real estate man with a seaplane. Rich agreed to fly into Bellingham and bring a mechanic, tools and a spare propeller to Crane Island.

The mechanic who came out with Rich was Dick Larkin. That was fortunate. Not only was Dick a master mechanic but he also was an older, no nonsense sort of fellow. I needed that. I evidently was so wound up that I just wasn't thinking straight. I was rushing around getting a propeller, etc, but what was I going to use it for, a boat paddle? No way could my airplane be flown out of that Crane Island hole!

Larkin, like everyone else including me, found it hard to believe an airplane had come through those tree limbs without striking a tree trunk… which were only 20 feet apart.

Larkin allowed himself one look, then got down to business. He lifted up the engine cowl. I said, "No Dick, it's the propeller." He ignored me. "Look here, he said, "This airplane is going nowhere." I looked. Every control and hose between the airplane and the engine was disconnected, shook off, broken. The two aft engine mounts were broken with the engine hanging down, supported only by the two front mounts.

Boy, I must have been really spaced-out to not have even looked into my engine compartment!

Schoen and family were on vacation. Using the second airplane, I continued to maintain the Company's scheduled flights. Several weeks later, after all the airplane parts had been accumulated, Larkin and his fellow mechanic, Bob Broberg, plus tools, came out of Bellingham to Crane Island by boat. The weather was hot and clear. That afternoon, between scheduled commitments, Bill Savage and I flew over in his seaplane to Crane Island, landing on the cove's little beach, directly below those terrible trees. The mechanics were doing great, in fact when we got there, they were just about done with their engine repair job.

Bill and I paced the length of the clearing. We could see the only possible way to fly the plane out of this 400 foot hole-in-the-wall was to go back out the same way I had come in… and I don't mean by another 'Hollywood' maneuver between trees. The line of trees that I had smashed through formed a towering picket fence between the clearing and the water. With limbs intertwined and trunks just 20 feet apart, it was, as I had experienced, a formidable 70 foot high barrier.

The Crane Island lady reluctantly gave us permission to cut down two trees, as long as we didn't disturb her 8-foot high deer fence that was nailed to them. I had not noticed the heavy gauge deer fence previously. By the broken limbs, it appeared my bottom wing had cleared the fence by less than 10 feet. Oh Momma me!

That evening the Savage boys and I discussed the pending Crane Island takeoff. It appeared, having only 400 feet of rough ground to accelerate on and an 8-foot fence to clear, I would need every advantage available. Bob Savage suggested I remove the wood propeller the mechanics had installed on the plane and replace it with his spare 'Aeromatic' adjustable propeller... which he would adjust for maximum power. His brother, Bill, suggested that in view of the high daytime temperatures, maybe I should delay the takeoff until the cool of the night, thus taking advantage of the extra lift from the cooler, more dense air. Good suggestions.

The next evening, after the day's flying commitments, Bill flew me over to Crane Island. The Savage propeller fit my Stinson perfectly. A full throttle trial run-up confirmed Bob's power settings. Carefully I taxied the Stinson to the far end of the clearing, Bill walking ahead checking for holes. Turning the plane around, we shoved it back under the tree limbs just as far as we could. Every foot would be crucial.

As the light dimmed, I hung a lighted kerosene lantern at the top of the deer fence, between the two fresh tree stumps. Standing at the fence I looked down on the little beach and at Bill and his seaplane. Bad place for Bill to be if I hit the fence. Bill was evidently thinking the same thing. He waved and departed.

I walked back across the clearing to my airplane, and waited. There was no wind. The air was sticky hot. The sea, the surrounding forest, silent, not a sound. I could just picture all the little wild creatures, hidden, hunkered down and watching, waiting to see what that roaring monster was going to do next. Well, like me, they would just have to wait. It had been a long day. I dozed off.

Awakening with a start, I turned on the dome light. The clock showed after 11:00 p.m. I stepped out of the plane, stretched and yawned. There was a light, wonderfully refreshing sea breeze touching my face.

From the other side of the clearing the lantern sent an unblinking challenge. It seemed terribly close.

I started the engine and pulled my seat belt tight.

Momentarily I flashed my landing light. No deer or livestock between me and the fence. I scanned the engine instruments, everything was normal. Turning off all the lights I waited for my night vision to return… using the time to plan my next moves.

To assure a margin of safety I should clear the lantern by 10 feet. That would mean the plane would have to be 18 feet in the air. Not very likely… not very likely.

With two trees chopped out… that gave me a 60-foot gap between tree trunks… probably 40, maybe 45 feet between limbs. Wingspan of my plane was 36 feet. Rough ground would throw the plane around. Must fly through the hole between the trees exactly in the middle. Nothing less than that could be accepted.

A limb impact would not stop me…

A trunk impact?

Think positive! Think positive!

Slowly I pushed the throttle to full power. As I listened to my engine (I know this sounds nutty) I involuntarily glanced to the left. I could almost see the deck officer out there, sweeping his wand towards the bow. Taking a deep breath, I released the brakes.

With engine howling, the plane leaped forward.

Just as I feared! The lantern was all over the place!

One moment it was lined up with the right corner of the engine cowl! Now the left! The center! Put the lantern in the center!

No more room! It had to be now!

I felt the tailwheel smack the ground as I rotated.

Breathing stopped. Somewhere back there in my mind a clock was counting; one, two, three, SMACK! A limb on the right wing!

Then nothing…………..

"I MADE IT!! I MADE IT!!

With Bob Savage's special prop in a real flat pitch, I couldn't fly very fast without over speeding my engine, but… BOY! Oh BOY! My wife and the Savage boys sure knew who just came over Friday Harbor, YES SIR, THEY SURELY DID!!

Needless to say, our two airplanes were immediately retrofitted with metal propellers.

How many feet or how many inches had my plane cleared the fence?

Nobody will ever know.

Following that Crane Island experience…. I kind of figured that God and I had come to an understanding; I'd fly em' and He'd give me a little boost whenever it was needed.

The arrangement worked great for the next 30 years.

CHAPTER 9

An Unplanned Landing on the Way to Olympia

In his later years, I noticed my Dad would invariably check the obituary column before laying his daily newspaper aside. I asked him if he was looking for someone in particular. "No," he said, "Just checking to see which of my old Army buddies have made the list." Pop was a World War I veteran.

So now my Dad is gone and it is I, a veteran of another World War, scanning the obituary columns. The passing of Mr. Robert Buck, a veteran of World War II, stopped me cold. For some reason I had expected Robert Buck to live forever. He was that kind of guy.

Thinking about Bob, as we all called him, brought back memories of a flight adventure that he and I once shared, some 50 years ago.

I'd like to tell you about it.

On this particular flight, I was flying a committee of three from San Juan County to our State Capitol in Olympia, Washington. Onboard with me in our four-seat Stinson landplane was our County Sheriff, Erik Erickson, our 40th District Representative, Violet Boede, and our County Prosecuting Attorney, Robert Buck.

Things in Puget Sound were in an uproar. My passengers were on their way to talk with the Governor. The situation was, the employees of the private Black Ball Ferry Company that served Puget Sound were on strike...

and had been for a week. Islanders were suffering; no ferries, no groceries, and so on.

That wasn't the only trouble we had... shortly after leaving the south end of Whidbey Island our engine sputtered and quit. It couldn't have been at a worse time. We were below a low layer of clouds, mid-channel over Admiralty Inlet, too far out to glide to either shore. Without an engine and with our airplane at full gross weight, we would be joining the frigid waters below in something less than 60 seconds.

I hurriedly switched fuel tanks. The engine tried... it sputtered, coughed several times and then went silent again.

Believe me, nothing sounds as silent as the sudden stopping of a roaring aircraft engine, especially when over a bad area.

Good heavens, it couldn't be the lack of fuel? We had only used 30 minutes out of full tanks. It sounded like water in the fuel.

This was confirmed a moment later when I bypassed both the sediment bowl and the carburetor and squirted a shot of gasoline direct to the engine with the hand operated primer pump. The engine immediately roared to life... for three or four seconds.

We had no choice; it was either the hand pump or swim.

BURRRP, glide, BURRPP, glide, each filling and emptying stokes of the hand pump took about six seconds. Each time the engine roared, our descent towards the water was momentarily interrupted. Two things were happening simultaneously... the tossing sea below and the shoreline ahead were each getting closer. Which would be the winner?

Sheriff Erickson was sitting up front with me; Bob

Buck the Prosecutor, and Violet Boede, the Representative, were in the back. This was Mrs. Boede's first airplane ride. Being deeply involved in discussion with Mr. Buck concerning the proposal they would make to the Governor, Mrs. Boede was totally oblivious to our flight situation.

At the time I was so sure we were going to make the beach that I thought, 'Why frighten the lady? The first she will know about the situation will be when we land on the beach.'

Instead... I should have had everyone digging their life jackets out from under their seats. I would realize this in something like 60 seconds from now.

Although involved in conversation, the Prosecutor was aware... (His father had been a World War I pilot). Sitting forward on his seat and turning towards Mrs. Boede, Bob Buck leaned against my back and while saying, "Yes Violet, I would agree with that " he whispered in my ear, "Are we going to make the beach?" I nodded.

We were making it all right... but when we reached the shoreline, OH, NO! There was no beach! The high tide had left only huge drift logs and boulders exposed. A water ditching? It was too late... my passengers were unprepared.

A few seconds more and we were staggering over what looked like an endless forest. The closest airfield was Bremerton, Washington, 20 miles away. We might just as well be on the moon for all the good it would do us.

Suddenly there was a break in the timber!

A little field! A farm house!

Instantly I knew the field was too small.

That couldn't be helped... almost anything was preferable to a deep forest crash.

With a last BURRRP of power we staggered over the treetops and dropped into the confines of the small clearing… our slow, staggering 70 mph suddenly seeming like the early morning express rushing into a tunnel.

The immediate thing staring us in the face was a rail fence that divided this small clearing into two pieces. Having no engine to break our descent, we hit the ground with a terrific downward force; the landing gear held and we bounced clear over that fence!

With what appeared to be a tremendous rate of speed and with very little area left, we bounced and careened through tall windshield-high weeds and brush, under the power and telephone wires bordering the driveway that ran to the house, banged through the driveway ditches… and that was the end of it. Swapping ends, we slide sidewise and came to rest with our right wing buried in a lilac bush alongside the house.

Mrs. Boede looked out the window for the first time and exclaimed, "My… Olympia has a rough airfield!"

An elderly Mr. and Mrs. Fredrickson came out on their porch and stood staring. The old fellow finally said, "We're sure glad you're all right. See that burned area by the trees? Those people tried landing here and they crashed and burned."

The Fredricksons invited us in for the use of their bathroom and telephone, in that order.

Using the phone, Sheriff Erickson made arrangements with the State Patrol for a car ride to the Capitol. It would be at least 45 minutes before the patrol car could arrive.

Mrs. Fredrickson immediately commenced making lunch for her unexpected, drop-in guests.

Mr. Buck was busy explaining to a skeptical Mrs. Boede, the whyfores and the wherefores of emergency landings.

I borrowed a fruit jar from Mrs. Fredrickson and went outdoors to check the airplane's fuel system. Wow! Both the sediment bowl and the carburetor bowl were full of water. Each of the airplane's fuel tank sumps still had some water!

Lunch was announced and shortly thereafter the State Patrol arrived. I assured my departing passengers that the flying company would have an airplane at the State Capitol in time for their return trip.

Violently rocking the airplane and alternately draining the tanks, fuel lines and sediment bowl (and after a good hard engine run-up), I was finally convinced the fuel system was free of water.

In the meantime, Mr. Fredrickson had filled in the driveway ditches with his tractor, knocked down some of the field brush and removed a section of the midfield fence. It was going to take all the room I could get to reach sufficient flying speed to climb up and over the tall timber.

Later that afternoon a good, favorable breeze came up. Being empty and light (I had drained most of the fuel out to reduce weight) the plane and I climbed up and out of that hole like a V-2 rocket. Circling back, I rocked my wings in salute to the two figures standing, waving, in front of the old farmhouse.

At the appointed time, I was refueled and waiting by my airplane at Olympia's airport when our three passengers drove up. They were pretty surprised to see me. None of them were very talkative. My attempts to relax them by joking and inviting them aboard "BURP BURP AIRLINES" didn't seem to go over too well.

Nevertheless, those people had that old-fashioned grit… they climbed aboard my little airplane, Mrs. Boede for her second flight ever. I flew them all home without incident.

The State took over the ferry system.

We tracked down our water/fuel problem to our Island airport gas pump and fuel storage system.

The Prosecutor gave me credit for a neat bit of flying for bouncing the airplane over that midfield fence. In those early Island aviation days we needed all the credit we could get... so I just smiled and thanked him.

He knew... you can't fool 'em all.

CHAPTER 10

A Tough Winter on Floats

That first summer, the summer of 1948, fled by rapidly. Unfortunately, the patronage on Schoen's scheduled route had not grown as hoped. As a consequence the airline did not need two pilots for the winter. Sure, last Spring the boss had warned me if business didn't improve, this could happen. Call it youthful optimism or whatever, I simply had not seriously considered the possibilities.

Now I was at the airport saying goodbye. The roar of Schoen's takeoff and his cheery words, "See you in the Spring," still ringing in my ears.

It wasn't until after Schoen and his airplane had faded in the far distance that I started to wake up to reality. Slowly I looked around. The empty hangar, the silent field... God, what a lonely place. What in heaven's name was I going to do? I was unemployed, broke. Winter was just around the corner. How was I going to support my young family through a winter on this little island?

That night, unable to sleep, I lay staring at the ceiling. An old Navy survival training film came to mind. It concerned a pilot who had either parachuted or ditched his plane in the ocean. Now, in his tiny inflated raft he sits staring as his squadron mates' planes fade into the distance. Even after the last rumble of their engines has faded away he keeps staring at the horizon. A voice on the film said, "No, they are gone. They cannot help you now."

Tentatively, the pilot looked around; nothing but

empty, lonely ocean from horizon to horizon. The voice continued, "Yes... you are on your own. What you do now, how you handle yourself, how you solve the challenges to come will determine the ultimate outcome. Take stock of your equipment and your situation; form a plan and get on with the program."

"Get on with the program." My recall of that old Navy film pointed the way; it solidified my thinking; got me on the ball.

In the meantime, the seaplane business was looking so promising that Bill Savage's brother Bob, also a single man and an excellent aircraft mechanic, had moved to Friday Harbor to join his brother. It was now Fall and a lot of the summer's seaplane activity was tapering off. With time on their hands the Savage boys put their heads together, thinking up creative projects for the winter.

Perhaps they were unduly impressed by the number of daily flights Schoen's landplanes had been making over the town? One way or another the boys came to the conclusion that a scheduled route is what they needed (they might have thought differently if they had known how many of Schoen's flights were being flown at a financial loss).

Anyway, the Savage boys decided to establish daily scheduled seaplane service between the Friday Harbor waterfront and the mainland town of Mt. Vernon, on the Skagit River. To accomplish this they bought a second seaplane and hired an extra pilot, me.

So now I was flying a floatplane, a three-place Piper 'SuperCruiser,' flying occasional charters and the twice-daily Mt. Vernon schedule. The new route seemed to have a lot of promise. From the Skagit River bank where we docked, to the Mt. Vernon bus station was just one city block. We visualized hordes of people welcoming this convenient bypass to the long and time consuming ferry

The Savage brothers—Bill (left) and Bob (right) at
Friday Harbor with Piper Family Cruiser

ride. Oh sure, docking the seaplane on a log boom in the
swift river current was a challenge, and jumping from
log to log and to the steep river bank was exciting... the
passengers would undoubtedly love it!

Day after day, flight after flight was flown and still

no passengers. "Not to worry," my employers assured me. "This possibility has been considered. Sufficient funds have been earmarked for the establishment of the route, however long it takes."

Brave words.

The weather turned wintry; the charter division of the Company was doing very little. Not so with the scheduled division; it was busily flying... empty airplanes, that is. Money was flowing in one direction only.

Tempers were getting a bit frayed. These normally happy seaplaners were no longer happy. I began to feel like the starving violin player who was saved by a rich man who hired him to play only for him. Like the violin player, it had been great for a little while... now I would give almost anything to be gone from this unhappy situation.

I didn't want to be a quitter nor did the Savage boys want to be quitters... however??

I did some checking around. The local Roche Harbor Lime and Cement Company needed a man. I told my employers I was about to leave. We remained lifelong friends. To my knowledge, the Savage brothers never tried a scheduled run again.

CHAPTER 11

Firing Lime Kilns at Roche Harbor

So now I was firing kilns for the Lime Company. The wages were more than I had been making as a pilot. Frankly, it sure felt good to just be a working man again and as the old Mississippi River song goes, 'sweat and strain, get a little drunk and you land in jail.' I didn't go quite that far, but now that we were no longer on emergency flight standby, we could, every now and then, hire a baby sitter for our one-year old, Steve, and join the happy crowd at the American Legion Club. We had almost forgotten how to dance. It was fun.

This company I was now working for, the Roche Harbor Lime and Cement Company, was by western standards a very old company. It had become and had literally remained for several generations a very important factor in this county's economy.

The production of marketable lime was what it was all about. Lime is obtained from limestone. To convert limestone to lime requires a tremendous amount of heat. The Islands had a wealth of both; massive deposits of high-grade limestone and miles and miles of forest.

The Roche Harbor Lime and Cement Company, under the ownership and management of Paul McMillan, developed into the largest lime producing company west of the Mississippi River.

I had never been involved with a large company before. I found it absolutely fascinating. There were so many divisions, each division separate and individual, but all contributing to the finished product. There were the crews in the limestone quarries, drilling, blasting and breaking the limestone (before heating, called green rock) into chunks of the desired size. The green rock was then loaded into railcars and moved down the tracks to the main scene of action. There the stone was dumped into bunkers which were directly above the blazing kilns.

In the meantime, independent woodcutters were out in the Island forests with their chainsaws, falling timber and cutting and splitting the logs into four-foot chunks of firewood, to fit the kiln fireboxes. Most of the woodcutters had their own trucks which they used to haul their day's effort to the lime company's wood yard. There the wood was stacked into cords (four feet high, four feet wide and eight feet long) recorded, and credited to the cutters. I was told the lime company kept a minimum of 1,000 cords in the yard at all times (if they ever ran out of wood and the kilns were allowed to cool, it would be a disaster).

Company employees trucked 24-hour supplies of wood from the wood yard to the firing areas and stacked it by the eight kilns. Each kiln was a separate, towering entity. They stood perhaps 40 feet tall, were skinned with steel, fire-bricked on the inside and were 12 or 14 feet in diameter. The uppermost part of their height tapered into the shape of a smokestack. They looked like a huge milk bottle.

Each kiln had two fireboxes, one on each side. The fireboxes were waist high to a man, fire-bricked and open to the interior. Access to each of these fireboxes was via a balanced, heavy insulated door.

Filled with green rock, the kilns were worked on three levels. The middle level was the firing level. The bottom level was where lime was drawn hourly from the base of each kiln and sent on an endless belt to the sacking department. Each time lime was drawn from the bottom; the whole column of rock in the kiln dropped six inches to a foot. A climb to the kiln's third level was required to draw enough green rock from the upper rock bunker to maintain the desired level in the kiln.

The firing of the kilns was almost continuous. Up one side of the eight kilns with their white-hot fireboxes, and then down the eight on the backside. The crews took turns, firing for an hour or so, then trading jobs with the men who were drawing lime and filling the kilns with green rock.

On my first day on the job the foreman took me over to a firebox and said, "Open it, inspect it and if it needs stoking, then stoke it." So I did. Wow! Talk about hot! I had stoked many a beach bonfire but this was white-hot heat. I picked up a snow-covered slab of fir and pitched it in, thinking to myself, 'this will never burn.' It almost exploded! Holy Mackerel Sapphire, that was hot!!

The maintenance people, powerplant people, the processing and shipping crews, the docks and ships, the office people and store people, all worked together. I actually enjoyed it.

Mr. McMillan was an influential man and he was politically active. Believe it or not, the then-President of the United States of America, Theodore Roosevelt, was a McMillan guest and stayed overnight in the company's Roche Harbor hotel.

But the years took their toll. By the winter of 1948, Mr. McMillan had died. The company was having a tough time. Accounts the company had had for generations were cancelling. The quality of Roche's product apparently was no longer up to standards. In desperation, Paul McMillan's wife and now manager of the company, brought in an efficiency expert. Among other things it was recommended that coal be burned along with the traditional wood. This supposedly would raise the temperature within the kiln and theoretically turn out a better product.

All I know is what the boss of our shift told us. In his opinion, the basic problem was the poor quality of the remaining limestone in the company's quarries. He thought the extra heat from the coal was accomplishing nothing and in the meantime was doing considerable damage to the kilns.

While working at Roche I had become acquainted with an old Russian by the name of Bill Kortenko. He and I worked the same midnight to eight a.m. shift. Bill was a slow, steady worker who very seldom spoke. From what he did say, I gathered he had never married and that he lived by himself in one of Roche's single man shacks.

One day old Bill stopped by my house in Friday Harbor. He said he wanted to talk to me. He said Roche Harbor had given him notice. They were letting him go. Would I please speak to the boss lady for him?

To my questions I learned he was 64 years old and could not draw Social Security for another year. I had never heard of old Bill being an alcoholic or a gambler. If he lived as I imagined he lived, he probably had lots of money squirreled away… yet here he was, really concerned.

It was during this conversation that I learned about Bill coming to this country from Russia when he was 29 years old. Except for the first couple of years, he had worked the entire time for Roche Harbor. With pride, he told me of all the brothers and sisters, nieces and nephews, who over the years had been Bill's extended family; whose problems and educations had been helped and furthered by regular contributions from 'Uncle Bill.'

With the income from his steady Roche Harbor job and the promise of the eventual Social Security check every month, Bill had not been concerned about the future. Now he was worried...

I really liked that old guy. I had no idea how I could help him but I promised to think about it and to do what I could.

Bill also had another reason for stopping by. He had heard I had some kind of connection with an airplane that flew every day from Friday Harbor to Bellingham. Could he go on it tomorrow and how much did it cost?

Several times a month during my Roche Harbor days off, I would fly as a relief pilot for Bob Schoen. Tomorrow was one of those days. The fact that we would be flying together tickled both old Bill and me.

Weather wise, tomorrow proved to be a miserable one... high winds and low clouds. Bill was my only passenger. When he and I were flying up President Channel to check Waldron Island's signal flag, we hit a mighty drop in the lee of Orcas Island's Turtleback Mountain.

Our flag system for landing on Waldron

As we dropped, the higher pressure in the cabin swelled the doors out by at least an inch and the air flowing past the cabin did the rest. The upper half of Bill's door broke outward and started banging on the side of the plane.

The boss was gone with our spare airplane. If we lost the upper half of Kortenko's door, this airplane could be grounded for days waiting for a replacement. Shouting over the roar of the wind, I prevailed upon old Bill to stick his arm out and hang onto the broken section. He did... but with a very concerned look on his face. I wondered if he was afraid.

While the door was being repaired and we were having a cup of coffee, I questioned Bill about his reaction in the plane. In his heavily accented speech he said, "I afraid... not for me... I old Man... I afraid for you... you young man with a family."

Back on the ground at Friday Harbor, I walked directly to a telephone and called the boss lady at Roche Harbor. I wasn't sure of what I was going to say or what Mrs. McMillan's reaction might be. Very likely she would tell this young upstart to mind his own business. Maybe she would even fire me for being so presumptuous. I could ill afford the loss of my job but I owed old Bill one; he had definitely touched me with his caring.

Mrs. McMillan's voice was clear and business-like. After identifying myself I broached the subject of Bill Kortenko's termination. She really surprised me by not cutting me off. I plunged ahead, telling her of Bill's steady workmanship; his years of service and of his financial need for one more year of employment. There was a silence, then she said, "As you undoubtedly know, the Company is having a difficult time. We are having to cut back on personnel. It has been recommended to us that we let the older, lower-producing people like Kortenko go."

Suddenly I had a brainstorm. My next door neighbor, Chuck Doyle, had been talking to me about the possibility of us buying one of those new-fangled chainsaws and finishing out the winter in the woods cutting and selling cordwood to Roche Harbor.

I leveled with Mrs. McMillan. I told her that in a few months I would be quitting and returning to aviation. However, I would quit immediately if she would let old Bill have my place. After a brief hesitation she gave me her promise to consider Bill's continued employment.

So... Chuck and I were now up on Cady Mountain and up to our hindends in snow. We soon found this Canadian chainsaw could indeed cut faster than the old manual crosscut saw. But when all things were considered, such as lost time going to town for parts, gas and oil, and the cranking and cranking required for freezing morning starts, perhaps my Dad's old manual crosscut saw wasn't that inefficient after all.

Chuck and I learned a lot of things in a short period of time. For one thing, we did not have a truck. Roche paid for wood delivered and stacked in their wood yard, not for wood sitting out somewhere on a mountain. We either had to buy a truck or hire someone with a truck to haul for us. One of the locals who was in the wood hauling business, Ted Schuman, agreed to buy and haul our output.

I'll have to admit there were some frigid mornings when I longingly thought of my nice warm airplane cabin. As of April 1, I went back to flying airplanes.

The Roche Harbor Lime Company lasted a few more years. By 1956 the quarry crews were gone. The hustle and bustle of the company town, the changing shift, the line of roaring kilns... silent... for the first time in three generations. Roche Harbor Lime and Cement Company was no longer in business.

An uncertain silence seemed to descend on the County. Some 300 people packed up and left.

For all those Roche operational years our local commercial fishermen had been able to fish the summer and fall seasons and be assured of making a good winter living cutting cordwood for Roche. Not now; the forest was silent.

A Seattle man, Reuben Tarte, bought the Lime and Cement Company and its assets. Reuben and his family began turning the little company town and its beautiful harbor into a resort. Miles of company owned shoreline were opened up for development.

Slowly at first, then later in a rush, people began arriving, buying and building. Many of these people were building homes to serve as summer cabins and later as retirement homes. These were new times at Roche Harbor.

CHAPTER 12

Arrival of the SeaBee

It seems strange now but in those first post-War years you could hardly find anyone in general aviation, mechanics or pilots, who had any pre-War aviation experience; at least in light aircraft. There were a few, like Jim Galvin of Seattle's Boeing Field, but Jim was the exception. So we of the World War II aviation generation had to learn the hard way.

We made a lot of mistakes. For instance, when Schoen's first Stinson Voyager reached 1,000 hours of flight time and the engine was due for its second overhaul, we all agreed the plane should be replaced. When the boss found a Midwest buyer for the poor old thing, we all gave a big sigh of relief. In later years we would think nothing of having a single engined airplane with 5,000 hours and more on it.

Bob Schoen with his friend and fellow pilot Eddie Lavender, departed with the 'worn out' Stinson for the Midwest; I kept the local schedules rolling. Bob told me later that while they were refueling in Lincoln, Nebraska, he spotted an interesting airplane parked there. It was a single engined, four-place SeaBee amphibian, practically brand new, covered with dust and dirt and obviously not being used.

That amphibian might have been forlorn and forgotten by its owner but its future was about to change. Instead of a ball of dirt, Mr. Schoen was visualizing that all-metal amphibian, all gleaming and beautiful, dancing across the sparkling waters of Puget Sound.

Bob was soon hot on the trail. The owner was contacted

and an immediate meeting was arranged. The SeaBee's owner was disappointed and disillusioned by the SeaBee's slow cruise speed and lack of small lake performance. Schoen was a guy who didn't let any grass grow under his feet. Shortly thereafter two people were heading west for Puget Sound in a SeaBee amphibian while another man was busily polishing his newly acquired Stinson; each man grinning to himself over the shrewd deal he had just made. I've got a sneaking hunch things didn't seem quite so rosy to either party by the time that 'sea-level loving' SeaBee had laboriously dragged her keel over the last Rocky Mountain ridge, or maybe when the new Stinson owner's mechanic prescribed a major overhaul for the engine. But, as they say,"That's the way the ball bounces."

Bill Savage was down on his Friday Harbor seaplane float pumping out the pontoons on his Piper when he saw one of those new SeaBees coming in. Like most hull planes compared to a floatplane, probably because of the additional hull area and weight, they plane longer before dropping down off the step. If a pilot is not aware of this characteristic he could bang the dock pretty hard. Apparently that's what was now happening to this SeaBee pilot. Muttering some unkind words Savage leaped up and ran to fend off the plane; maybe even save his own plane from damage.

Just as Savage leaned his body out, arms extended to help absorb the shock, Schoen shifted his propeller into reverse and poured on the coal. The SeeBee stopped and began to back up. Savage, with his eyes getting big and round and his fingers missing the nose of the plane by inches, slowly fell flat on his face into the frigid, salty brine.

Such was San Juan's County's introduction to the SeaBee era and Bill Savage to reversing propellers.

Since I had some previous seaplane experience flying for Savage, and since the largest population center in this island archipelago was the waterfront town of Friday Harbor, where I lived, it was therefore decided the SeaBee would be my baby.

I hope the reader has taken into consideration that this was a new and untried 'aeroplane.' So buckle up and hang on!

With this amphibian, as a daily operation, I picked up people and dropped them off from Friday Harbor's city float. For overnight security I flew the SeaBee empty, out to Friday Harbor's cow pasture airport.

To keep the Bee, as we called her, neat and clean and to minimize salt-water corrosion, a daily fresh water bath was required. Unfortunately, fresh water was not available at the cow pasture... so very shortly we moved the plane to Fat Wilson's shipyard area where water was available. That was the summer of 1949.

One little problem: on the shipyard shore next to a fresh water spigot, right where I wanted to park the Bee, was an interfering accumulation of drift logs. Fortunately, the yard had a young man down there doing a job for them with his bulldozer. This young fellow's name was Fred Sundstrom. Like most guys of my generation, Fred was intrigued with flying machines and so was more than happy to push the logs out of the way.

That shipyard setup really worked great. After landing on the water I would approach the beach, pump the landing gear down and as the wheels touched bottom and the hull started rising, I'd give her the power and up we would come, high and dry!

The hull had five compartments, each one drained by a threaded plug in the keel. At the end of the day I'd remove the plugs, drain any accumulation of salt water and then hose her down inside and out. At the beginning of the day I'd put the plugs back in (only forgot once), check the plane over, taxi down off the beach until we were afloat, pump up the landing gear and tear down the harbor, on the step, to the town's waterfront.

I liked that harbor trip... both ways. It's where I developed my famous 'Salmon Leap.' Throttled back, planing along about 50 miles an hour on the step, I found by pushing down hard on the nose and then popping the control wheel back, the Bee would momentarily leap clear out of the water. Just like pushing a cork underwater in the bathtub! Very spectacular! I could make three of those leaps between the shipyard and downtown. Great advertising! "Come fly the skies with Island Sky Ferries!"

Loading and unloading the SeaBee while it was in the water was a misery; the airplane's wingtip floats prevented the plane from getting in alongside the docking float. Also, having a boat hull instead of pontoons there was nothing to step out onto. However, the 'Bee' had a unique nose door. That's right, a nose door. This was made possible by the airplane being a pusher and not a puller; the engine and propeller being mounted behind the cabin, not out in front. Half of the windshield served as the door. With only half an instrument panel and the airplane in the water and securely tied, it was possible to step right from the dock or float directly into or out of the airplane.

Securely tied, right? If you were free floating and looking for a place to unload it was okay if you had someone in the co-pilot seat who could jump right out through the nose door and secure the plane... which wasn't very often. Can you imagine telling the sweet old grandmother sitting there, "That's right sweetheart; just jump right out there and grab that greasy piling before we drift away!" "Now look at you! You should have jumped farther."

Docking was only easy when there was someone on the boat-float who knew how to help. This helper would pick up your wing and if there was enough room, pull the wing and plane in until the hull was against the float. This of course put your wingtip float up on the deck, meaning someone had to walk your wing back off when you wanted to leave. Solution? Have a float designed just for the Bee, or... have a ramp that you could taxi up on with the wheels.

In the meantime, we had some flying to do. On this particular day it was hot and Bob and I were inbound to Bellingham with the morning schedule. Bob was flying the Stinson; I was flying the Bee. I don't remember who Bob's passengers were on this particular flight but mine were three members of the Allen family from Eastsound.

The big advantage of an amphibian is of course the ability to use whichever is the handiest, water or land. Since our only downtown car was based at the Bellingham airport, the airport was naturally our desired point of landing. As the Bee and I came into the airport traffic pattern, things started to get complicated. Selecting gear down I started pumping the required hand pump. Just as the pump was coming up to needed operating pressure, the handle went slack. I glanced out through the side windows; my main landing gear wheels were still up. Damn it! A hydraulic system failure.

As they say down at the Chinese laundry, "No tickie, no laundry." All same, "No landing gear, no landie...right?" Ah, but this was an amphibian! I called the boss on the radio. Schoen said, "Put her on the water." He would swing by the waterfront with the car and pick up my passengers.

When he heard this over the cabin speaker, one of my passengers, Sparky Allen, exclaimed with enthusiasm, "Oh good, I've always wanted to experience a water landing!"

With the hydraulic system not functioning we not only had no landing gear but we also had no flaps. It was a hot morning with no wind and the Bee was at full gross weight. With no flaps she would have to be landed at a bit higher speed. I wanted very much to do this right. Not only were the Allens, as far as I was concerned, special people, but there was also such a thing as pride in workmanship, right?

I lined up on an open piece of water that was close in to a downtown dock. The air down by the cool water was as smooth as silk. I smiled to myself, anticipating Sparky's exclamation of, "Really? You mean we are on the water? Why it was so smooth I never even felt it!"

Flattening her out I waited for that feeling of drag, of smooth deceleration... heralding, "Another perfect landing!"

Wham! Bam! The nose tucked down, the hull slammed the water, the plane bucked up and down violently and the windshield came partly out of its rubber molding.

I was stunned! Good Lord, how could I have fouled up the landing that badly?

Sparky said, "Hey that was fun! I thought it would really be rough!"

Slowly I taxied over to an empty float, my mind going over and over the landing, searching for a logical solution.

What had I done wrong?

Mechanic Chuck Edwards came down with some hydraulic fluid and a flaring tool. The hydraulic line running from the cabin area, down to the aft hull and back to the tailwheel was broken. I did not know this at the time but in the Bee's system sequence, the tailwheel went down first, then the main gear. I had gotten just enough pressure into the hydraulic system to put the tailwheel down but not enough to unlock the main gear. With no cabin indicators and the tailwheel out of view...WOW! It's a wonder it didn't jerk us in two!

Pretty soon I saw Chuck hanging over the side and losing his cookies. I said, "What's the matter?" He said,

"Inside that hull it's over 100 degrees and the bottom is filled with your spilled hydraulic fluid."

"So? I said.

"Try hanging head down in that oven with those fumes in your face and with the whole damn thing rocking!" After another spasm of 'errphing' he continued, "I don't know whether I got a decent flare on that tube or not. Better check it."

I pumped the gear down and up; seemed to be okay. By this time the boss was back and said "Okay Roy, I've only got two people going back out, I'll take care of them. You run out with the Bee and bring in those Waldron people who were booked later." "Aye, Aye!"

Everybody departed. I untied the Bee, gave her a good shove and climbed in. Blankety! Blankety! Blank! I had forgotten the battery would not turn over the engine when the engine was hot! Thanks to the manufacturer who put the engine on the back and the battery up in the front, there was too much line loss, especially for a tired battery. To reach the propeller on this machine for a hand-start, one had to duck under the wing and then squeeze between the fat cabin and the protruding, retracted landing gear leg and wheel, all the while balancing on the narrow hull protrusion. Then you had to reach up with one hand to the backside of the propeller blade and give it a good hard downward pull. Rotation of the engine required this to be done on the pilot's side of the plane.

At the moment there was another problem: if I succeeded in getting the engine started, the plane would run into the dock pilings before I could get into the cabin and control it. There appeared to be only one solution… paddle back to the float. It was one thing to step down onto a seaplane pontoon and paddle, quite another with this rig. Getting the paddle out of the anchor locker and using both open sidedoors, I dug water on one side and then the other. God, what an awkward thing! Like trying to paddle a car. With sweat pouring, I finally got back to the float and secured the airplane. Time was slipping by. Unfortunately, I had the wrong side of the plane next to the float, but there was no time to correct that. Crawling across the cabin I stepped out on the waterside, onto the hull protrusion and squatting down under the wing, I started aft between the cabin and the retracted landing gear leg.

Good Lord! I never thought to have the parking brake on. The instant I put my weight on the wheel it spun and I fell face down in the lovely, sewage filled harbor.

To make a long smelly story a bit shorter I got that sucker started and for the next several hours flew passengers while barefoot and wet. I didn't mind that so much, it being a hot day and all, but as my sewage bath became a bit ripe the passengers' comments became less and less complimentary.

You know, all this negative talk about the Republic SeaBee is a little embarrassing. Actually I enjoyed flying the Bee and I flew it on hundreds of perfectly satisfactory flights... but you would never guess it by the way I talk about the poor thing. I think a Factory Rep said it best. He said, "If the factory had spent more time perfecting the airplane and its equipment instead of trying to jump the post-War civil aviation boom with a radically different and unproven airplane, then instead of having to shut down SeaBee production in just a matter of months they very well could have had a winner and been in production for years."

Well, that's all well and good but the fact of the matter was, we owned a SeaBee and were trying to make a living with it. To enhance the plane's usage, the first thing we were going to do was build a special float for it.

At this particular time, mid-winter of 1949-1950, the town of Friday Harbor's small boat facility consisted of nothing but a relatively short, single line of floats, secured by driven pilings and running straight out from shore. There was no breakwater. Permission was granted for us to secure our new SeaBee float on the outside end of this city float.

The new float creation we had dreamed up was built in the shape of a U. This allowed the Bee to taxi straight into her nest. On departure, utilizing her reversing propeller, she could back out just like a boat. The side-fingers of the new float were narrow enough that the plane's wingtip floats straddled them. This put a walkway on each side of the hull, convenient to the Bee's big, auto type side doors.

The Bee's new docking float worked great except for one thing; the plane bobbed and rolled like a cork every time someone stepped in or out. You guessed it; those big, lovely open doors of hers crashed down onto the float-deck at every roll.

So it was back to the nose door after all. Actually, with the plane tightly snuggled up in the end of the U, the nose door worked out very well.

One night, a week or so after installation of our new SeaBee float, a raging Noreaster storm struck. At daybreak the next morning, stumbling along the waterfront's shoreline, bundled and mufflered against the biting cold, I stopped and stared in disbelief; the city float and all the boats secured to it, our new SeaBee float... all gone! Fortunately, the Bee was securely lashed and safe at the shipyard.

I searched the shoreline, hoping to at least find some of my cedar logs and planking. Nothing! The only thing visible was a pair of boat hull-planks with an inboard engine attached staring up at me from the depths below. That was all. My God, Friday Harbor needed a breakwater, BAD!

CHAPTER 13

Some SeaBee Misadventures

This next episode was not the Bee's fault. It was caused by my own inexperience.

It was now getting into winter and the challenges of keeping the SeaBee operational were increasing. On this particular day the temperature was not only dropping but it was beginning to blow from the northeast. The forecast called for a pretty severe storm by nightfall. Schoen was off-island and out of touch for a few days. I had several loads of passengers in Bellingham for Waldron Island and had only the SeaBee to do it with.

A northeast wind on the old Waldron runway was a quartering tailwind. By the time I arrived over Waldron Island with my first load, a downwind landing with the Bee on the island's short, steep, uphill airstrip was already out of the question. Nor could we land on the wild, exposed water at the foot of the runway. I was therefore left with two choices: either go back to Bellingham and cancel all flights, or... land the people on the water on the far side, in the lee of the island.

These winter storms often blew for days. If we cancelled, these people could be stuck on the mainland for a week or more. On the other hand if I landed them over on the lee side, which would be several miles from their cars, two of the passengers, Emery and Alvita Johnson, who were elderly, would find it difficult going. Perhaps I could land in the lee of Point Hammond near the airstrip, then taxi on the water around the Point and put these people up on the beach at the foot of the runway. That would put them just a few hundred yards from their cars. It was worth a try.

Wow! Taxiing around the Point and into the wind— and into those seas was really something! I'll say one thing for the Bee, she might not have been the greatest flier but she was a pretty darn good boat! Putting the gear down and roaring up onto the beach worked fine. Unloading in that freezing wind was something else again; it just about took our breaths away! The instant my passengers were clear, I fired up and started angling down off the beach. The waves had the water so riled up I couldn't see what was down under there; rocks, soft spots or what, so I took it very slowly. Just as the hull started to float the Bee came to a stop; the right wheel was up against a big boulder.

It was a critical situation. The storm seemed to be increasing by the minute. I knew if I didn't get free of this situation immediately, the waves and this rock were going to do the Bee in.

Lots of roaring, pumping the control wheel, kicking the rudder; nothing worked. Finally, when a bigger than usual wave picked the plane up, I retracted the gear. Granted, a wild thing to do... but I was desperate. I figured the Bee and I had just a few more waves before the destruction would begin.

Oh Lordy, it worked! I was free! Slamming across the waves and up into the sky, I headed for Bellingham. So I figured I had the secret, 'retract the gear the instant I had floating depth.'

By the time I was back with the last load of passengers the situation with the wind and the seas was getting pretty marginal. No question about it, we were in for a real old-fashioned winter storm.

We made it onto the water and around the Point, through

the seas and up onto the beach. Got everybody out and on their way. Now for the water re-entry. Slowly taxiing down off the beach, I made sure to avoid that rock. A wave picked the plane up and I started retracting. Bang! It sounded like something broke back in the hull. Good Lord! The landing gear was floating limp on either side of the plane! I had hydraulic pressure but it wasn't doing anything...

Each succeeding wave was pushing the plane back higher on the beach. I looked in the bilge. A clevis that formed the connection between the actuating piston and the landing gear was broken. I couldn't fly the plane with the gear dangling. Jumping out into the freezing water, I ran up the beach to a log that had some rope on it. Bringing the rope back to the plane I tied one end of the rope onto one gear leg, threw the rest of the rope over the cabin roof and looped it around the other gear. On the Bee the two landing gears are connected so heaving up on one gear leg raised both. Although I didn't get the gear up as far as it would be in its normal up-flight position, nevertheless, it was high enough. With some frantic pushing and shoving, plus some roaring, the Bee and I were up and away.

Where to land! With no landing gear I didn't want to make a belly landing at Bellingham Airport. The waterfront? Considering this storm, the Bellingham waterfront was too exposed. With no maintenance shop, Friday Harbor was also out. That left Bellingham's Lake Whatcom. The lake would be well protected by the surrounding hills and it was only four or five miles from the airport maintenance shop. I landed on the lake.

Chief mechanic, Earl Erickson, drove out to assess the Bee's damage. That broken connecting clevis between the power cylinder and the landing gear was the problem. A new clevis would have to be ordered.

It wasn't hard to see what had caused the problem.

The clevis was strong enough to raise and lower the gear but was not meant to hold the entire weight of the plane. When the wave picked the plane up, I started the retraction cycle. I wasn't quick enough. When the wave rolled on by the plane dropped down on the partially retracted gear. Bang!

A real 'doozer' of a storm was developing. I called Margaret Ann in Friday Harbor to let her know I was still in one piece and wouldn't be home for several days. "How were she and the children doing?" She said they had plenty of food and were all staying warm and just praying the Island's underwater power cable didn't go out. She added that the trees in the yard were thrashing and the harbor was a sea of white caps and wind streaks.

Fortunately a gear clevis was found in Seattle and we had it by noon the next day. Lordy, it was cold working down in that aluminum hull! Several hours later I was ready to go.

Crunching out through the fast forming layer of ice on the lake to open water, I took off. Boy oh boy! A 30 or 40-knot tailwind all the way home! At Friday Harbor the winter winds and high tides had earlier blocked the shipyard beach with drift logs so I had moved my operation back out to the cow pasture. Now when I touched down on the pasture the Bee started to decelerate rapidly and to tuck its nose down like the brakes were on. Then with a veer to the right and then to the left, it straightened up and was okay. Until now I hadn't noticed. Taking off from the fresh water lake the spray had locked my wheels and gear legs into a cocoon of ice!

As far as I was concerned, I had had enough SeaBee flying for now and figured it was time to go home and see the wife and children. Climbing into my '36 Ford, I hit the commencer; nothing happened. I lifted the hood… Good heavens! I had just had the radiator overhauled and was going to buy the anti-freeze in Bellingham (because I could get it cheaper, right?) The engine was frozen up and busted wide open! It cost me a month's wages for a re-built engine block.

"Live and learn," as my mother would say.

"But Mom, why does it have to be so darned expensive?"

The Bee and I flew nearly every day for the rest of the winter... but eventually it happened. The oil pressure on the Bee's engine was going down and the temperature was going up. With no aircraft maintenance in the Islands, the boss said to limp the Bee, if possible, into Bellingham. I did. The shop drained the Bee's engine oil, along with a handful of internal grindings.

It was the early spring of '50 before the Bee was ready to try out her freshly overhauled engine, her new rapid reversing propeller and her new slow turning auto type ignition system. I don't know what it cost, I was afraid to ask. I had the feeling though, one more problem with that amphibian and she would be history. She was not the boss's favorite moneymaker. With all the improvements, the Bee was becoming a much-improved airplane. In fact it was now a pleasure to fly.

Margaret Ann with young Steve and the SeaBee at Shipyard Cove, on a nice calm day in 1949.

But sadly, a few months later came the final trouble. It was Friday evening and we had, it would seem, half the population of San Juan County wanting to fly from Bellingham to the Islands. Bob was again flying the Stinson; I was flying the Bee. Coming back empty to Bellingham for another load, the hydraulic system on the Bee suddenly went slack. The main gear was still up and according to the newly installed wing-float mirrors, the tailwheel was down. Dirty name!

The boss asked, "How much fuel have you got?"

"Two hours," I replied.

"Okay," he said, "Circle there at Bellingham until I get these last two loads out. When I get back, we'll put her in on her belly alongside the runway."

"Aye, Aye."

It would take Bob about an hour to run those loads out so I had plenty of time to think. I wasn't concerned about the outcome. By this time, Republic Aircraft's SeaBee had been operational for several years. Consequently the ability of the Bee to withstand belly landings on dry land, intentional or otherwise, had been tested many times.

During my hour of circling I recalled reading about a B-25 bomber prototype at the beginning of the war which ended up doing exactly what I was doing now, circling and circling with a gear problem. At the time, because of the world situation, the U.S. needed that plane very badly. After all engineering suggestions had been exhausted and as a last resort, the flight crew was told to use any liquid— coffee, anything to get that gear down. Very shortly thereafter the gear came down and the plane landed. The plane's captain wrote on the check-off sheet, "I recommend this airplane be given a complete urinalysis."

Remembering that story didn't help my situation, however. While the boss was busy flying passengers, the boys from the maintenance shop were also busy. Walking through the tall grass alongside the runway they scouted out and marked with a line of white lime the place for me to put the keel. They also removed all the rocks they could find that might cause damage to the belly of the plane.

Eventually the boss was back and was now down there by the runway analyzing the situation. I was surprised when with swinging arms he indicated the opposite side of the runway from the mechanic's chosen spot. Too bad; I found out later there was a lack of communication. Anyway, the boss was saying, "Put my plane here" and that's where I put it.

The air was still and although I had no flaps I was lightly loaded. The Bee went on smoothly, decelerating steadily and as the weight of the plane came down off the wings and onto the keel and tailwheel, the keel cut an ever-deepening V groove in the sod. The plane came to a stop balanced perfectly on its hull; neither wing-float had touched or was now touching the ground.

Cars came thundering up with backslapping congratulations. I wasn't listening. I was too busy cleaning out the anchor-locker and inspecting the inside of the hull. The congratulators were unaware the plane had stopped with a grinding jerk.

It could hardly have been worse. A big boulder that was flush with the top of the ground and not seen by my boss was now protruding through the broken keel and into the hull.

A young man about my age and driving a new pickup truck with Alaskan license plates, turned to Earl Erickson, shop foreman, and asked, "What will it cost to fix the landing gear and the damaged hull and keel?" After taking another long look, Earl said, "$500.00."

As I said, my boss wasn't one to waste time messing

around. Evidently the Alaskan was cut from the same cloth. The dickering was short and to the point. In no time at all Schoen was driving off in his new pickup truck and the Alaskan stayed to supervise the raising and the repair of his newly acquired SeaBee.

That's the last time Island Sky Ferries ever considered owning or operating a SeaBee amphibian.

CHAPTER 14

To Aircraft Mechanic School

The winter of 1950 was approaching. Air traffic on our scheduled routes, especially during the off season, was still not that great. I was again faced with the strong possibility of a winter without employment.

Bob Schoen had recently sold his scheduled Air Service to Dave Howarth, an ex-military pilot who had moved to San Juan Island. I had flown steadily through the Fall, then with winter coming on, there was no need for two pilots, so I was out of a job.

Decision time. General aviation was my thing. I could fly 'em but I couldn't repair 'em. If I was going to make this my life's work and had ambitions of still being alive 10 years from now, then it was time I learned how to maintain my own machinery.

I still had some eligibility remaining on the GI bill. The decision was made; we would move to the mainland for the winter and I would enroll in an aircraft mechanic school.

The school I wanted to attend was located at Arlington, which is about 40 miles north of Seattle. Arlington's airport had been a Navy training base during the war. The mechanic school's classrooms, restaurant, etc. now occupied a number of the Navy's former buildings and hangars. Students who were single were housed in the old steam-heated military barracks. My family and I occupied the married couple's apartment in this same barracks building. For assigning rooms, checking people in and out, etc., we received our quarters rent-free.

Besides the mechanic courses, the school offered a flight program. Since I had a flight instructor's rating and the school needed flight instructors, it all worked out just great. Uncle Sam paid for my mechanic schooling, plus $90 a month living expenses. The before school, after-school and weekend flight instructing provided the rest of the needed family income.

The mechanic course was divided into two separate programs, airframe and engines; I chose to take engines.

This going-back-to- school was fantastic. My class-mates and I were all veterans and we were there to learn. It was a thoroughly enjoyable experience. Two of the students from Alaska became my lifelong friends. One was a jolly bear of a man, Cy Hetherington, from Manley, west of Fairbanks. The other was a powerfully built, happy Eskimo, Rod Lincoln, from Kotzebue, north of the Arctic Circle.

Weather-wise the winter of 1950-51 was a tough one. That bad winter caused some drastic changes in the Island aviation picture. As the new owner of Schoen's Island Sky Ferries (the name had been changed to IslandAir), Dave Howarth had had enough. He shut down his island operation and moved back to the mainland. That meant the Islands were without scheduled air service... and for me, it meant I would have no flying job waiting for me in the Spring.

With a wife and two little children to support and no prospect of a job in the Islands, I thought seriously of staying with the school as a flight instructor and signing up for the second part of the license, the airframe part. That idea evaporated when I found out the school was in the process of closing.

A telephone call from a Mrs. Ferris of Orcas Island changed everything. This lady, Virginia Ferris, and her sea-captain husband, Harold, and their daughter, Janet, lived on a farm on the north shore of Orcas Island. The Ferrises owned an airplane and had built a little graveled airstrip right there on their farm. That airstrip of theirs was now being used by the local airline; or was, until the airline shut down.

Harold (Cap, everybody called him) was at sea 80 percent of the time with his Matson Steamship job. In his absence his wife Virginia and daughter Janet ran the farm, the airport, took reservations for the airline, and so on. They were busy people. The Ferrises were understandably concerned when the one and only island airline shut down.

Over the years of working for Schoen and then for Howarth, flying in and out of the Ferris airstrip, my family and the Ferrises had become good friends. Now Mrs. Ferris was calling on the phone to ask about my wife, Margaret Ann, and the children; how was I doing at the mechanic school and what were my plans for the future?

I said something like, "With no operating airline in the Islands, if a person could raise the capital, it would seem to be an opportune time to resurrect the old airline."

She answered, "Yes, Harold and I have been talking about that!" Don't ask me how those two communicated… he, out on the Pacific Ocean most of the time, no satellite communications in those days and yet there it was, "I'll speak to Harold about that; yes, we were talking about that!"

What she said next just about knocked my socks off… "Would you consider," she asked, "Going in with us on re-establishing the airline? Harold and I would put up the required money; you would run it and we would help you in any way we can; you could use our airplane."

"WOW! What a great idea, Virginia!" "Is this airline idea for real, Virginia? What does Cap think about it?" Her answer… "It is real if you say yes!"

I tell you boys, I just felt like sitting down on my haunches and howling at the moon!

"Dear lady, you have got yourself A DEAL!" "Wonderful, Roy! Harold will be so happy to hear this!"

After we each got our breath back, Mrs. Ferris continued, "Why don't you come and pick up our airplane and take it to the school? Harold will not be needing it for several months. "I'm sure you will want to do a lot of work on it before using it on the schedule."

I did just that.

Although the school and the flight instructing kept me very busy I did fly the Ferris Stinson several times during the remainder of the winter. The most interesting flight was when I flew the Ferris daughter from Orcas Island to the southern Oregon port of Coos Bay… and back.

Mrs. Ferris had been keeping her husband company on board his ship for several weeks as he moved the ship from port to port, unloading incoming cargo and reloading cargo for the next outbound trip. Sometimes she would drive the family car from port to port… other times the Captain would have the loading crane pick the car up and set it on the ship's deck for a port to port piggy back ride.

Now the ship was at Coos Bay, its last U.S. port of call before departing.

It wasn't very often that Mrs. Ferris had the opportunity to accompany her husband to distant foreign ports… but this time she was sailing with him clear to the south seas and beyond to Australia. Both he and she wanted to see their daughter before they left. They called me and asked if I could pick Janet up on Orcas with their airplane on Saturday morning, fly her to Coos Bay, stay overnight and then fly her back to Orcas on Sunday?

Hey! Hey! With the Captain paying all the bills and a

chance to see his ship… I was tickled to do it.

The Ferris daughter was a bouncy, happy high school kid, the weather was ideal and the beautiful booming surf of the Oregon coast was magnificent. It was a great trip. Cap and Virginia met us at the Coos Bay Airport with their car and we all drove to Cap's ship which was busily loading cargo at the waterfront.

Watching a ship being prepared for a sea voyage is always fascinating. The smell of the salt water, the dockside hustle and bustle, the cry of the gulls; it really quickens the pulse.

After going aboard, the Captain said, "We have several hours before our dinner date, what would all of you like to do?" I immediately said, "Captain, I would like to explore this ship of yours from stem to stern." There was a momentary silence. The captain's wife then drew herself up and looking him right in the eye, said, "In all of these years, Harold, I've never been below deck on any of your ships; I think a tour of the ship would be fun."

Daughter Janet joined in with a resounding, "Oh, let's!" I could tell by the sudden flashing of the eye and the working of the jaw that this was not at all what the Captain had in mind. In a thundering authoritative voice he said, "You may go below and crawl through every hatch and rat hole you can find, Mr. Franklin, but no wife or daughter of mine shall go below the top deck of any ship that I command."

There was a total silence, save for the gentle lap of the water on the hull and the squeak of the loading winch. It occurred to me to make some sort of remark but the thought of the rack and the cat of nine tails stayed my tongue.

After clearing her throat several times, the Captain's wife said, "Well, now that we have that settled, let's all go into the galley and have a cup of coffee."

Later, onshore and over a very nice restaurant meal, Janet's parents gave us an interesting summary of their pending South Pacific voyage. It all sounded mighty adventurous and intriguing!

The big topic of discussion, however, was of course our upcoming springtime joint airline adventure. This was the first time the group had had a chance to discuss the subject face to face. I had some nagging concerns; maybe Cap and Virginia had done some reconsidering?

No by heaven! They were as eager to get started as a couple of kids! No second thoughts, no doubts; full speed ahead! WOW! WOW! WOW!

The next morning Janet and I flew northward, she, returning to her Orcas Island High School and me to my Arlington mechanic school. Well, that is at least how the flight plan read… but this old bus of Cap's had other ideas. About 30 miles short of Orcas Island our ignition system was suddenly running on just one magneto. A few minutes later the one remaining magneto failed and we started down. Fortunately, the first mag failure had given me enough warning to have a cow pasture picked before the second and final failure. This old engine seemed to be giving me fair warning; like, "If you plan on restarting an airline with me, you had better get your maintenance program on the ball."

Responding to my telephone call, one of the boys from the school flew out with tools and picked us and the two faulty magnetos up. Janet went home to Orcas via bus. I retrieved the plane a few days later.

CHAPTER 15

Reconditioning a Stinson

So now it was April 1951. With a crisp new 'Aircraft Engine License' in my pocket, the family and I were in the process of moving back to the Island. There was no time to lose, we had just two weeks until May 1, the date we had chosen for the restart of the airline.

One of my biggest immediate challenges was the condition of our one and only airplane. Frankly, the airplane was in pretty sad shape. One thing, the machine was still in the same old 1947 configuration as when she originally came from the factory; that, plus some years of mighty hard usage.

The owner of the plane, Sea Captain Harold Ferris, enjoyed flying but he was never on land long enough to really get very skilled at it. Consequently, with no aircraft maintenance facilities anywhere in the County, the airplane had been continuously used, unintentionally abused and put away wet, as they used to say. I had longed to work on the airplane while still at the school but with short daylight hours, no place available to work undercover and... with the continuing inclement winter weather...it just wasn't possible.

The gods must have been smiling on us because almost to the day of our island re-arrival the weather turned to clear skies and sunshine. It's amazing the effect sunshine has on a person's spirits, right? Even the sad condition of Cap's airplane couldn't put a damper on the joy I felt in being back on the Island, of working on a flying machine amid the sunlit peace and quiet of a country flying field.

Making a detailed assessment of Cap's airplane was number one. It started with one beat-up wood propeller, no spinner, bald tires, cracked wheels and worn out brakes and landing gear oleos, battery kaput, no anti-cow-manure wheel fairings, worn-out tailwheel assembly, fabric coming loose around the fuel tanks—and the whole airplane, its red finish oxidized into a miserable dull orange. Then there was the engine, a no gyro instrument panel and a non-functioning radio.

I had two weeks. I ran an estimate past the Captain's wife; she gulped and said, "Have at it!"

Since Margaret Ann was expecting the arrival of our third child at any moment, she was unable to take part in our airplane restoration. Sooo... with 4-year-old Steve and 2-year-old Susie signed up as 'helpers,' the family and I headed for King's cow pasture airfield and Cap's flying machine.

We did all right. In between the oh's and ah's over the latest crawling bug or worm discovery, the children scrubbed on the fuselage's oxidized paint while Papa started on the engine.

At lunchtime Mama came out, and spreading a blanket on the grass in the shade of the plane's wing she invited the children and me to join her for a picnic lunch. We certainly didn't disappoint her, no siree. As lunch progressed Mama and I exchanged knowing looks over a couple of nodding heads and soon she and the two very weary little tikes were on their way home for a well-deserved nap.

After determining that the compression and the basic engine was sound, I installed a set of new spark-plugs, replaced the starter and generator with factory overhauled units, checked the freshly overhauled magnetos, re-timed the engine; installed a new battery, new metal propeller and spinner, tires, brakes, wheels, fluid and seals in the landing gear oleos and a new pneumatic tailwheel assembly (not all in one day).

The fabric work, matching of paint, painting of the scrolls and company name (Island Sky Ferries), the manufacture of wheel fender brackets, radio work and the installation of a turn and bank gyro—all that was accomplished in Earl Erickson's Bellingham aircraft maintenance shop.

I had two days left. Using what they called, ' dope-rub,' I cut the old oxidized finish on the plane down to its original beautiful color, then gave the whole airplane a Simonize wax job.

May 1st arrived bright, clear and beautiful. I'll tell you no lies, when the Ferris Stinson rolled out of the hangar and into the sun that morning, she literally glowed! Fact is, from her glittering silver propeller and spinner to the company name bordered in lovely scrolls down her flanks… to her streamlined wheel fenders and her new, large, pneumatic tailwheel… she was really something! There was no question about it… she was a beauty! And you could tell just by the way she stood there that she knew it! She certainly did.

"So," I said to this lovely lady, "If you fly as great as you look, you are going to be a real winner." I was not disappointed.

The only land plane fuel available in San Juan County at that time was at the Ferris airport on Orcas Island. As I landed and taxied up to the fuel pit on that May 1st morning of 1951, Virginia and Janet, not wanting to miss the inaugural flight, came hurrying down across the pasture from their house. Cap was at sea. All of us were really thrilled over the restarting of the airline!

Incidentally, this day was my 27th birthday.

I wondered what these two women were going to say about the airplane. They stood staring for a few minutes, whispering, then Virginia approached my fueling ladder and looking up, said, "I know you had an awful lot of work to do on our airplane, Roy. This is a most beautiful airplane. Where did you get it and are we renting it until you can get our plane finished?"

I said, "Take a look at the 'N' number, Virginia." She did and her gasp and exclamation made those weeks and midnight hours of work all worth while.

YAHOO!! THE AIRLINE FLIES AGAIN!!

CHAPTER 16

Getting Busier With More Stinsons

May 4th, four days after our inaugural flight, Margaret Ann gave birth to our second daughter, Janet Pauline. Mother and baby were doing fine. Our house was filling up. The wonderful thing was ... all members were healthy and happy! The newest member was a little sweetheart. The first thing we saw in the morning was her big smile. Life was good.

Air service wise, the next 24 months were incredible. By this time every other island flying outfit which had tried flying a schedule had given up. I was bound and determined that that was not going to happen to us. Being the company's only pilot, in fact the company's only employee, it meant a seven-day a week effort. Adopting Bob Schoen's philosophy, "Come hell or high water, fair weather or foul", I flew the schedules... on time and every day.

It didn't take long to realize that night maintenance with a flashlight held in the mouth cannot keep up with the airplane that is being flown slam-bang in and out of cow pastures seven days a week. We needed a second airplane as a maintenance backup. My Ferris partners agreed with me.

We purchased the second aircraft from Flight Craft of Portland, Oregon. Being happy with the 1947 Stinson Voyager model, we made sure both our airplanes were nearly identical. By standardizing on parts, engines, propellers, tires, brakes, instruments, radios, etc, we were able to keep our investment in spare parts inventory within reason and yet still keep enough on hand to limit maintenance downtime.

Margaret Ann with her sister, Pauline, at King's Field, about 1950

The addition of the new plane, N-9047K, made life so much easier. The Port of Bellingham built our company an open hangar attached to the side of Bellingham Flying Service's aircraft maintenance shop. We kept both our spare airplane and our downtown limo in the new hangar.

Things were starting to click! For the first time our limo was being kept under cover. No more iced or snow covered car. Any airplane problems and I could limp in, trade airplanes and be gone in a matter of minutes. No loss of time; the shop would take care of my sick one. Great! Great! Great!

However… we soon found that two airplanes were not enough. When the Captain was home he wanted a plane for his own use, right! Couldn't blame him for that. With one plane in the shop and myself flying the other, the unhappy Captain was afoot.

We could not find another Stinson Voyager so we had to take what we could get. The third Stinson, N-306C, was what the factory called their 'Station Wagon'. It had wood paneling on the interior walls and a 165 hp Franklin engine instead of the 150 hp as in the two Voyagers. The Station Wagon model was very popular with Flying Farmers.

In the meantime, things were beginning to move hot and heavy. Not only was the doctor using the airplane more and more for his medical evacuations and for his neighboring island sick calls, but after a successful bid we were now flying the summertime fire patrol in the Cascade Mountains for the Mt. Baker National Forest. Thrown into this boiling brew of activity was the steadily increasing patronage on our scheduled routes and the daily charters for the local telephone and power company crews. Fortunately those crew flights were flown before and after the daily schedules.

It was wearing but elating; people were finally recognizing our little airline as a legitimate means of travel. I was weary and tired but I was not the only one on this seven-day a week treadmill. Each and every day Margaret Ann arose before dawn, making sure my day started with a hearty breakfast and that I left with a packed lunch under my arm. As long as we could keep our eyes open, the two of us had our eyes on the future.

High aloft above the mountains on midday fire patrol; that's known as dining in a noisy restaurant with an aerial view! Only thing lacking—no little boy's room and no props for the eyelids.

By this time, 1951-1952, most of the GI flight schools had faded out of the picture. With the demise of those schools, training planes were a drug on the market.

Cap's and Virginia's daughter, Janet, wanted to learn to fly. For a few hundred bucks Cap bought a two-seat Aeronca Champ. So now my daily dance card was not only filled with schedules and charter flying, but mid-day mountain flights and student work. It left not a moment to spare. The packed lunch saved my life.

Like most well coordinated, sharp kids, Janet took to flying like it was second nature. At this moment, her father, the sea captain, was home on a break from his high seas duties and as usual was bursting with months of pent-up energy. I swear, when that ruddy, red haired, compactly built sea dog hit the beach you could almost see a track of burned rubber left behind him. No question about it, the Captain was a man of action.

My concerns over the narrow gravel runway and the girl's low hours of experience didn't hold much water with the Captain. "Damn it, if the girl is ready, then solo her!"

As Janet taxied the Aeronca Champ down the runway and out across the summer-dry marsh, I looked behind us and there was the Ferris automobile driving out and parking in the grass, facing the middle of the runway. It would be Cap and his onshore buddy, Harold Jensen. They would be there to have a little snort, share a few sea stories and enjoy the airshow.

Perhaps it was because I was still smarting from yesterday's cross-examination or perhaps it was like James Cagney of the movies who used to say, "That's the kind of hairpin I am." Whatever the reason, when we reached the end of the runway and Janet turned the plane around, I started to chuckle. Janet glanced over her shoulder at me and asked, "What's so funny?" "Your Dad," I said, "is sitting in that car bragging to Harold on how perfect a takeoff his daughter is about to make." Janet nodded and said, "So?" "Because, my dear young lady, your Pappy is about to witness the damndest takeoff he will probably ever see." With that I said, "I've got it," and releasing the brakes I shoved the throttle wide open.

Swerving from side to side, levitating one instant then slamming back on the ground the next, we rapidly approached the car. Now for the grand finale! In an apparent out-of-control situation, one wheel up in the air, the wing tip dragging through the grass, we headed straight for the car. The car made one convulsive leap forward then shot straight back into a deep ditch; rearing up into the sky like a V-2 rocket about to be launched. We zoomed up and over.

The longer Janet and I stayed out in the practice area, the more I was assailed by self-incriminations and regrets. How could I have done such a stupid thing? For every good flying job there were half a 100 hungry guys standing in line. Stupid! Stupid! Stupid!

The gas gauge began to tell us we must return to the scene of the crime. When we did, there was no sign of the car or of anyone. I began to wonder if it had really happened.

I flew the scheduled roundtrip to Bellingham. On arrival back at the Orcas Airport I found a note pinned on the bulletin board. "The Ferris family," it read, "wishes your presence at their home, P.D.Q."

"Oh Lord!... Well, I've done it now."

With leaden feet I slowly walked across the intervening sheep pasture to the Ferris home. I wondered how he would do it? Blazing eyes and curses? Or, cold as ice and finger pointing at the door, "Never to darken forever more!" Christ, if I was on his ship it would be the cat of nine tails... no, it would probably be, 'Walking the plank!'

With dread I climbed the 13 steps to the kitchen door. To my hesitant knock Mrs. Ferris swung the door open with what seemed to be a non-committal, "Hello Roy," her finger pointing towards the living room.

I had only taken a few steps in that direction when Mrs. Ferris said, "Harold got a young deer last night, so we are having liver and onions... thought you might like some." Mrs. Ferris was a very gracious woman but as I thanked her for her thoughtfulness I couldn't help thinking, "the condemned man was being given his final meal."

In the living room Cap was telling one of his ocean adventures to a rapt audience of friends. A delicious odor was wafting up from the liver and onions sizzling on a grill in the open fireplace. Either the Captain didn't see me come in or he was choosing to ignore me. Perhaps he would not embarrass me in front of these people? One way or another I made myself as inconspicuous as possible. That wasn't hard to do. Cap's tales of the sea were fascinating and everyone's attention was riveted on the storyteller.

I relaxed just a mite.

I love fresh venison liver with onions, especially when it has been harvested during the late summer before the rut; a month or so before hunting season. I was not disappointed, it was simply delicious! Everyone was so friendly and relaxed that I was soon swept up in this feeling of good cheer.

It therefore came as a tremendous shock when suddenly and unexpectedly I had a face to face confrontation with the Captain. His eyes bored into me as he spoke in a low and private voice, "Were you the one making that takeoff today?" I choked and blew out a piece of onion that stuck to his nose. "YYYes sir," I stammered. Cap stood very still, his sea captain's eyes piercing me like radar. After a long, long moment the Captain reached up, brushed the onion from his nose and with, " I thought so," spun around and rejoined his guests by the fire. WHEW!

Eventually Captain Ferris returned to the sea and life for the rest of us returned to a more normal pace. The incident with the trainer takeoff was never mentioned again. Over the ensuing years I made a conscientious effort to put a damper on my impulsive tendencies—with varying degrees of success.

CHAPTER 17

Go or no go?

Winter, with its rains and howling winds, was upon us. Operationally, there was always that decision, "to fly or not to fly." Of course if it was really howling, there was no question. The difficult decisions were the ones that concerned the weather for tomorrow morning. If we waited until morning to make the decision not to fly, our stranded passengers would have also missed the morning ferry. On the other hand, if we cancelled tomorrow morning's flights on the strength of tomorrow's forecast, more than once the Pacific storm would stall out on the coast and we would fly around all morning with empty airplanes.

During that particular era, many of our morning passengers were traveling to keep mainland optical, dental or medical appointments; some appointments made months in advance. These people were our friends and neighbors. If a severe storm was approaching the coast we would call each of tomorrow morning's passengers and say, "It doesn't look good for the morning flight; we think you had better plan on taking the ferry."

Varying reactions, of course. Most often it was, "Oh darn, well thanks for calling. I've had that eye appointment for two months so I guess I'd better take the car and go. Sure hate to though; that ferry makes it an all day trip."

There was always that balance between trying to play it safe, make a living and still provide a scheduled service that people could rely on.

Then there were those passengers like the two ladies from Orcas Island. I guess I'd better tell you about them. They were something special. Fact is, I'll tell you about the whole flight; it will give you a peek at some of our so called 'challenges.'

So here it is. By this time my family and I had moved across town to a big old rambling two and a half story house up on the hill overlooking the harbor. One morning I groaned as a gust of wind rattled the old house and limbs on a tree outside the window of the upstairs bathroom thrashed wildly. Darn! I was hoping the forecast would be wrong. As I hurriedly finished shaving, the beep, beep, alert-signal on the old low-frequency radio sounded, followed by Fred Cook's reedy voice with the quarter-after-the-hour weather from the Bellingham Flight Service Station. As his voice droned on I stepped up onto the rim of the bathtub and looked out the small bathroom window, watching as a gust of wind spilled to the surface of the harbor. Boats, like weather vanes, were tugging at their anchor chains and pointing their bows into the rising southeaster.

Darn it! This would make the third storm in three days! Last night on TV they said there was a line of vigorous storms all lined up like soldiers out there in the Pacific, marching in to hit us, one about every 24 hours. Well it sure looks like they called it right.

It wouldn't be so bad if the timing was different. The way it had been, and it looks like it's going to do it again today, the storm front will approach all morning with a rapidly falling barometer and an ever increasing wind velocity. About mid-afternoon, with a brief swirl of rain, the front will pass, the wind will momentarily drop, the sky behind the front will break into sunshine and the wind... the wind will find its voice again and come roaring back, now from the southwest, feeding for a few hours into the backside of the receding storm.

But what really takes the cake is what has been happening the last two nights and in all probability will happen again tonight. I've come home tired and beat with that miserable wind still whipping the trees. But then after supper as I walked downtown to the Fire Hall for my volunteer fireman's training session, the wind has been calm and the sky beautiful and clear and filled with a myriad of twinkling stars.

I've only one comment. It is mighty hard to make a living with a little flying machine when the air is so rough that no one wants to ride. Wouldn't it be just as easy to have it nice during the day and storm at night? I swear, sometimes I think nobody is listening!

I gingerly feel my sore belly and bruised kidney areas. After two days of stormy weather flying, of fighting into and out of little airstrips, crosswinds spilling and swirling the air like water over a rapids, it leaves my center section feeling like I've been in the ring with Joe Louis. Heaven knows I don't relish the thought of another day of it. As I descend the stairs the heavenly odor of bacon and eggs wafts up to my eager and twitching olfactory department. The timing is perfect; my bottom touches the chair seat at precisely the same moment wife Margaret Ann slides my loaded plate before me. Great service! Great breakfast! The thought occurs to me, as I busily demolish my breakfast, maybe we could buy a little fast-food joint, which my wife could operate, and then I could retire? I verbally explore this possibility but between rushing from stove to table to stairs, calling up to the children to hurry, trying to find their school books, fresh clothes, etc., my dear wife doesn't seem to think I'm very funny.

Seizing hat and coat, I dive into the melee and grab a little goodbye kiss, whispering a sweet nothing in her ear.

Reaching for her trusty broom she says with a chuckle, "Get out with you, that's what got me into this circus in the first place!"

Laughing, I sprint for the door. "Bye kids," I shout. From every level and corner of the old house it seems, little voices call back, "Good bye Daddy," "Bye Daddy," "Bye bye Daddy."

At the airport I stand for a few moments in front of the old open hangar letting the wind buffet me as I take its measure. Low scud clouds race by. The windsock, rigid with pressure, whips and saws back and forth on its mast. Somewhere on the hangar a piece of metal is flapping.

While untying the plane I look at my watch; 20 minutes to scheduled takeoff. Carefully I inspect the airplane, check the gas and oil, pull the prop through, push the plane out of the hangar and start the engine for its warm-up. The gusting wind makes the plane tremble and shake. "Don't blame you a bit," I say to my little airplane, "If I didn't have people booked out of Orcas I'd probably put you right back in the hangar." Talking to my airplane always makes me feel better, particularly if I'm not sure I'm doing the right thing.

During the warm-up I debate—to go or not to go, that is the question. The Company has a total of two airplanes. If half the fleet is destroyed on this flight it would probably put the Company out of business. If I'm still around I would be out of a job. On the other hand if I start cancelling out for every little windstorm that comes along, the Company's fragile economy could be permanently fractured.

I turn on the radio and listen to Bellingham's latest observation. Scattered scud at 500 feet, 1,000 overcast, visibility 5 miles, wind out of the southeast at 25, gusting to 38, barometer falling. Not too bad, I thought, ceiling and visibility should hold; falling barometer is the wild card;

just how far it will fall and how strong the wind will get is the question.

I make the pre-takeoff run-up. Everything checks out. Shutting down the engine I carefully lock the brakes and walk into a dark corner of the hangar for my last minute nervous pit stop. Oh Lordy, that old wind sounds mean as it buffets and bangs the hangar!

Back in the plane I fire up and check for traffic. Traffic? HA! That's a laugh! Who the hell besides this numbskull would be out in weather like this? Sometimes my caustic self-observations have a good influence but not today; evidently we are going flying. "Okay sweetheart," I say to my little red Stinson, "Let's go!" Fighting the gusts I hold the plane tight to the ground until we have solid flying speed, then we fling wildly upward into the teeth of the gale.

Cautiously turning downwind in the turbulent air we head for Orcas Island. Enroute, I'm thinking of the flight ahead and of my two elderly Orcas ladies, Mrs. Harry Fowler and Mrs. Allen, who are waiting to fly to Bellingham. Lordy, I hate to subject those two nice older ladies to the wild ride I know Mt. Constitution has in store for us.

But what can I do? Mt. Constitution rears up out of the water to a height of 2,500 feet right on our course from Orcas to Bellingham. With a high ceiling we would have two choices, the slow, long and fairly smooth route around the mountain on its windward side or the shorter but violent leeside route. Unfortunately the low ceiling today negates the advantages of the windward route.

During these ponderings I had flown halfway up Orcas Island's Crow Valley, and WHAM! I hit the air turbulence flowing from Willard Mountain. One moment the safety belt is trying to keep me connected to the falling airplane, in the next instant the rising airplane meets my descending body with a grunt. Well actually it was me who grunted, the airplane just creaked and groaned.

By the time I was on the ground at the Orcas Airport the wind was approaching gale force and I had made up my mind about the two ladies. Reluctantly leaving my pitching and trembling aircraft, I hurriedly made my way over to their car. Mrs. Fowler rolled down her window part way and asked, "Are we ready?" Pressing close I said, "Ladies, this is not the day for an airplane ride. We will be happy to rebook the two of you in a few days when the weather has calmed down." I was sure these women would be greatly relieved by this announcement. To my amazement, they didn't appear to be relieved, in fact they actually looked disappointed!

With the wind whistling past my ears I couldn't hear what they were saying to each other in the car but after a few verbal exchanges it was evident they had come to an agreement. I leaned down to hear what Mrs. Fowler had to say. She asked, "Are you going through whether we go or not?" "Yes, I've got a load of freight to bring back." "Then we will go with you," she said. "But ladies," I protested, "It's a wild and stormy day! If you go now you may never want to fly in a small plane again!" The ladies looked at each other for a moment. I saw Mrs. Allen nod. Then Mrs. Fowler turned to me and asked, "Will it make any difference to your plane if we go with you?" "No, no problem there, but…" "Good, then we will go with you! Don't worry Roy," she added, "We won't be afraid." I looked at them for a long moment. By George, they really did look determined!

As we slowly and cautiously taxied downhill and downwind prior to takeoff, I briefed my two brave passengers on what to expect.

"Right after we leave the ground we will encounter the first big drop; followed by a hard upward push. I will be expecting it so don't let it worry you. Just let your hands rest naturally in your lap; don't grab hold of things; try and stay relaxed; roll with the motion like riding in a small boat. If you can stay relaxed you will not experience the dropping sensation that bothers a lot of people."

After takeoff, although I flew far downwind in an attempt to be as far away as possible when we crossed the mountain's wake, it still proved to be more violent than I had anticipated.

All during the worst part of it my two rear-seat passengers kept up a steady chatter. I could hardly believe it! Here I was, fighting the controls, being hammered down in the seat one moment, hanging on the belt the next and those two little old women were sitting back there talking away like a couple of magpies. Unbelievable!

As soon as we were past the influence of the mountain and the air was smoothing out a bit, I turned around in my seat to congratulate my two intrepid flyers.

The sight that greeted my eyes was really something! The two were sitting there facing each other, eyes tightly closed, gripping each other's hands and both talking at the same time! I shouted, "It's all right ladies, you can open your eyes now!" The two of them stopped talking but their eyes remained tightly closed. "Are we on the ground yet?," asked Mrs. Allen. I laughed and said, "No, not on the ground yet, but the rest of the trip will be better." The two ladies didn't budge. "If you would be so kind as to let us know when we are on the ground," said Mrs. Fowler. "Okay I will, but you ladies should open your eyes and look around, especially if either one of you feels air sick." No reaction from the ladies. Glancing over my shoulder a little while later I was happy to see both my passengers were looking out the windows. They were still tightly holding hands, however.

Calling Bellingham Radio on my one frequency transmitter I asked Fred for the current wind. "Sustained winds at 32, gusting to 48, occasional gusts exceeding 50, barometer starting to bottom out, no reported traffic," was his reply.

There would be a time in the future when I would have accumulated enough local weather knowledge to enable me to make some reasonably intelligent go-or-not-to-go decisions. Right now I was still learning. The fact the Company survived these learning years would have to be credited to a lot of luck and to the benevolence of whoever 'up there' is in charge of the aviation department.

It seems rather unbelievable now but Bob Schoen's little airline was the first post-war 'Airtaxi' in the entire United States to fly a daily posted schedule and survive. He wasn't the first to have the idea but his little outfit was the only one started in early 1947 that was still operating years later.

Stormy weather grounded all air activity at Bellingham Airport… except for United Airline's several DC-3 flights and the arrival and departure of Island Sky Ferries. That meant students and instructors were crowded into the coffee shop and flight offices; bored and staring out the windows hoping to see something more exciting than the usual rain and scud clouds.

With the sound of the approaching Stinson from the Islands, the wilder the weather the more interesting the air show promised to be and the most active the betting. I know because I used to be one of those coffee shop observers.

Today, coming in over the airport, the wind was sliding us sidewise about as fast as we were making forward progress. Boy, that ought to get a few bets going!

Entering the airport pattern and turning downwind I had to immediately turn onto base leg and then onto final or be swept out of the traffic pattern entirely. Wow! The side drift was really something.

Still at our pattern altitude, we were now over the runway and lined up. In normal winds we would be way too high to make the runway. Not today. Slowing the plane down and lowering my flaps, I tried to hold an airspeed of 70 miles an hour and a sink rate of 500 feet per minute or less. Now that we were faced into the wind our forward progress over the ground appeared to be almost zero. We were making like a model airplane in a wind tunnel, droning away and going nowhere! Which was fine; exactly what the doctor ordered! A slow controlled sink to the runway below.

My two lady passengers were about to see another reason for this early Company's survival; it was the eager and interested, volunteer participation by almost everyone.

Down there on the edge of the runway a car was just now dropping off two men. Alerted by telephone to the situation by Fred from the Flight Service Station, these men, Earl Erickson, shop foreman, out in the middle of the runway ready to catch my right wing; Bill Southern, flight school instructor, ready to catch my left wing. Without their help the chances were pretty remote of my taxiing this lightweight, tailwheeled aircraft in this wind across the open sweep of the airport from the runway to the protection of the buildings without suffering a flip over.

Bringing the plane down to the runway surface, with a few skips, I got the main gear on the runway surface and with the tail still up in the flying position, taxied slowly and carefully toward the waiting men. As we came up to them they each took a few running steps and seized hold of our wing struts. Cautiously letting the tail down, we slowly moved off the active runway and started the long taxi to the Terminal.

At first all of us were pretty tense. Even with the men putting their full bodyweight on the struts the plane would heave up hard in the gusts. Fred and his radio shack were about a quarter mile away and directly upwind from us. Every time a gust hit the shack, Fred would call a warning. His warning would just give me time to stop the plane and set the brakes before the gust would travel across the open field and strike us.

It was slow work, but as the effort proceeded without incident we all relaxed just a trifle. Bill Southern, on our left wing, was a natural born comedian and he started doing some hilarious stuff like hanging by one arm while scratching and grinning like a chimpanzee. After the rather hairy ride my passengers and I had just experienced, Bill's antics really cracked us up. Our reaction, of course, gave Bill encouragement for further stunts.

Bill had false teeth and one of his favorites was to remove them and holding them out at arms length, clack them at you; all the while his eyes would be dancing and his rubber face would be folding up and swallowing his nose! He was right in the middle of this act, hanging by one arm, when a sudden gust smacked us. Fred must have been out of the radio shack taking a weather observation or something. At any rate, the gust hit us without warning. At that precise moment I was looking right at Bill. The plane heaved up off the ground probably not more than a foot but the suddenness of it scared the daylights out of us, particularly the guy who thought he was going for a one-armed airplane ride.

After that Bill got real serious about walking his wing. We proceeded across the remaining exposed area without further incident and soon had the plane tied down in the protected lee of the buildings. I drove the ladies into town and dropped them off in the shopping district.

The storm front passed through the area by mid-afternoon. The sky cleared and the shifted wind blew itself out in a few hours. By the time I flew the ladies home that evening the sun was shining, the air was smooth, the Islands and the sea looked fresh and sparkling clean. What a beautiful sight! What a difference a few hours can make!

It has been said, "One cannot fully appreciate the beauty of the valley until one has first faced the trials of the mountain."

I turned in my seat and looked at these two spunky, lovely, elderly ladies. Yes, I would say Mrs. Fowler and Mrs. Allen had faced the mountain. They could be on my team any old time they wanted to be!

CHAPTER 18

A Thousand Passengers, a Thousand Stories

One of the benefits of piloting a small, I mean really small single-engined airplane on what would eventually be called a Commuter Airline, was the fact that the plane's interior was so small that you ended up literally rubbing elbows with your passengers. A thousand passengers, a thousand memories. Some wanted to talk; some wanted to ask about the names of the islands passing below us, some were busy with their thoughts.

I remember one young woman travelling from Orcas Island to Bellingham who had just been told her father had died suddenly and unexpectedly. She was devastated. She sat there trying desperately to control herself, the tears streaming down her face. I reached over and put the back of my hand against her cheek; she squeezed my hand between her cheek and shoulder for the longest time, and the poor kid wept and wept.

One time a big bear of a man with a friendly grin squeezed into my little airplane. I recognized him immediately. I said, "What do I call you, Mister? or John? Or what?" He said, "My friends call me Duke." I thought about that for awhile and then said, "Seeing as how you have spent more time in the last 10 years in my family's TV room than I have, would you object if I called you Duke?" The big guy grinned and said, "Sounds good to me, Pilgrim!"

Then there were people like old Ed Chevalier who had

spent a lifetime in these islands, enthusiastically pointing out and naming just about every rock and shoal visible from our aerial perch. To Ed I asked, "How is it you know all these things?" He chuckled and said, "At one time or another, I've hit just about every one of those things with my boat."

It's amazing what you can see from an airplane, right! One time I said to a farmer passenger "Looks like you missed cutting the hay in the corner of that field? "Yeah, you would notice that wouldn't you," was his embarrassed comment.

One time on Waldron Island, an isolated community of less than 100 people, an old bachelor by the name of Mark Hays made the Air Service quite an offer. He told me he would paint a white cross on the top of his black car and if I ever brought anybody into the Island who needed ground transportation, just look for the cross and give him a buzz (with the plane, that is, there were no telephones on the Island). Sometime later, after this offer of his had temporarily slipped my mind, I whistled by his place just to say hello and Mark took off with his car for the airport. We decided after that, maybe I shouldn't be so friendly.

On one particular morning flight from Bellingham to the Islands I had two passengers, a young woman for Orcas Island and an older woman going to Friday Harbor. Under the circumstances I couldn't bring myself to just fly the young woman to her destination. Fortunately it was one of those flights where Mother Nature was at her best: a pod of Orca cruising along by Lummi Island, a pair of bald eagles soaring, a mother seal and her pup on Parker Reef. With our engine throttled back and slowly circling, we observed without disturbing.

When we eventually arrived at the Orcas Airport the young woman came around the airplane and gave me a hug.

I messed around with the baggage compartment door for a minute or so until I had regained my composure, then slid into the pilot's seat. The older woman said rather severely, "What was that all about?" Swallowing hard I said, "Last night I flew that young woman and her little boy to the hospital. The little boy died. I wanted to remind her with this flight that God is still in His heaven.

I didn't know it at the time but that older woman was a writer of stories for magazines. The story of our flight later appeared in the *Ford Times*.

Then there was the handsome Orcas islander, Stan Englehartson, single, bashful and happy. Anybody with that big a smile must have been happy, right? Then Stan met a Swiss miss from Switzerland who was with a visiting class in Moran State Park. (I might get nailed on this but come on now, that's the way I remember it, okay?) Anyway, the point of the story is, this lovely young woman flew with me to Seattle to catch her plane back to Switzerland. I was remembering Stan's anguished face at the Orcas Airport when they said goodbye. She had hesitated... and hesitated... but old Stan just couldn't say it. So that was that. She was on her way home.

The next thing I knew, this Swiss miss is booked on my very next return flight from Seattle to Orcas Island; leaving, say in 20 minutes! Holy Mackerel, old Stan had paged for that girl in the Seattle-Tacoma International airport terminal and told her he couldn't live without her... and now she was rushing back to save his life. YAHOO!

When we landed at Orcas I didn't have the engine shut down yet before Stan had the door open and that girl in his arms, WOW! "Hey! Hey!" I say, "take the belt off and leave my airplane here!" They sure did love each other! Still do from what I hear.

All kinds of little daily adventures. Jack Boyce and

Bert King were working for the San Juan County Road Department. Their assignment for the month was running a rock crusher on the south end of Lopez Island. Both of the men lived on San Juan. At the time, Lopez had no airport so I was flying the two men, morning and evening, in and out of a cattle pasture near the crusher. The owner of the pasture, Ted Richey didn't mind but he had one huge old bull who did not agree with the arrangements at all. When it gets right down to it a person really couldn't blame the bull. There he was, in isolation, cut off from the herd, only called in when one of the cows desired his company. Nobody thought to ask him what he wanted. It was enough to make any old male grouchy and cantankerous. On top of that, here came that noisy, lousy airplane—painted red!

So that old bull stood right smack in the center of his field, pawing up the ground and every time I started a final approach, here he came, 90 miles an hour! I'd have to pull up and go make another approach. While I was making the circle mister bull would retire back to his centerfield position and await developments. Couldn't help but admire the old boy.

After twice being denied entry, something different was needed. Again... flaps down, slow approach... Yep! Here he came! So instead of going straight ahead and up over him, we stayed back and did a quick circle. That suckered him clear down to the fence. Boy! I think he figured he had scared us real bad! Flipping out of the turn, we hopped over him and landed.

Chuckle, chuckle, sure fooled that old bull! Coasted on over to the far fence where the men had their truck parked. The first man got one leg out of the airplane door and, "LOOK OUT!" here came that damned old bull, head down, charging! My engine was still running; slamming in full power I kicked the tail around into the bull's face, expecting to take the impact in the aft section and not into the cabin. Nothing happened. Cautiously throttling back, I took a look. There he was, walking away, shaking his head as if to say, "Blowing dirt in one's face is not fair!"

Shortly thereafter the farmer called upon the old bull for services that only he could perform. Duties over, he returned to his pasture a new bull. Come to think of it... maybe he was? One way or another he had a grin from ear to ear and our previous territorial disagreements were then forgotten.

Talking about it later, Jack Boyce shook his head and said, "That was a lot of bull!" We all agreed. Yep, we surely did.

CHAPTER 19

Some Humorous Incidents

With the beauty of the Islands framed by a magnificent sunset, I flew towards Orcas for my final pickup of the day. I smiled as I thought about my Dad. After a long day of work, shocking hay, picking spuds or whatever, when we finally got to the last one he would shout, "Here's the one we were looking for!"

This flight was like that. It had been a long day. I thought about the men I was going to pick up at Eastsound—loggers who flew with me every morning and evening. There was big and jovial Bud Wold, six foot three and 276 pounds. There was quiet and steady Tony Surina, and then there was Junior Hodson who would much prefer to keep a minimum of one foot on terra firma.

I chuckled just thinking about this trio... good natured, hard working men, logging up on Buck Mountain for L.D. McIntyre; men who always had a humorous little event of the day to laugh about... such as the bulldozer taking off and sliding down the side of the mountain with the operator hollering bloody murder.

The more I thought about these fellas and their sense of humor the more I chuckled and the more I chuckled the more I thought of pulling a good one on them. For the life of me I couldn't think of a thing until my eyes fell upon the old gin bottle filled with battery water, sticking out from under the back seat.

Ah yes... the old drunken pilot act!

Yep, there they were, standing down there with their empty lunch boxes; waiting.

Oh Boy! Oh Boy! Oh Boy!

Yo-yoing up and down, burping the engine like a World War I Spad, I came in fast, smacked the runway with the wheels, followed by a mighty aerial bounce; more bursts of power, waggles of the wings, a screech of rubber off the runway and a wild taxi up to the three statues; finishing with a reckless, roaring, sliding flourish.

Crawling out of the plane with a silly grin, gin bottle dangling by its neck from a limp hand, I fell back against the plane and after a heavy burp, said in a slurred voice to the bunched up and silent loggers, "What do yah say we go for a little old airplane ride."

After a long, stunned silence, big Bud stepped forward and snatched the bottle from my hand; he sniffed it, then poured some in the palm of his hand and tasted it with his tongue.

"Oh for Christ sake," he said, "It's water! Nothing but water!"

Tony said, "Give me that," and snatching the bottle from Bud, he went through the whole procedure, sniffing, tasting and finally declaring, "Water, that's all it is, just water!"

All this time Junior was suspiciously eyeing both the airplane and me as if to say, "That pilot might be fooling but not that damned fool airplane!"

Junior's inspection of the bottle and its contents took so long we were all in the plane waiting while he was still sniffing and tasting. By this time we were all in gales of laughter.

As we flew into the sunset somebody started it off and we all joined in, "Row, row, row your boat gently down the stream," all except Junior; he was still suspiciously sniffing and tasting that bottle of battery water... all the way to Friday Harbor!

When operating an airplane in and out of an active cow pasture as we were doing, one of the many things we had to contend with was of course the catttle themselves. On a long, hot day it happened. We bashed one of those bovines!

Big Bud was sitting up front with me, Tony and Junior in the back. If the cattle had been scattered all over the pasture as they usually were, then by buzzing I would have herded them off to the side and out of the way before making our landing. In this case the cattle posed no problem as they were all on the far side of the pasture; all except one which was evidently enjoying the cool of the hangar's shade.

The grass runway at Friday Harbor went up and over a knoll, the crown of which was about 150 yards from the north fence. Our one-plane hangar sat on this knoll, the runway passing by just 50 feet from the open hangar entrance. In landing, it was convenient (and fun) to drop down low, skim over the north fence and touch down against the knoll's upslope, providing of course, the wind and the 50 or more resident cattle cooperated. Often with cool air and a light load, I could land, brake down and turn right into the hangar.

On this day, having a heavy load and the thin air of a hot August afternoon, we would be needing most of the runway. Suddenly, just at touchdown, a cow came streaking out of the open hangar, tail up in the air and on an exact 90-degree collision course with the plane. Full throttle, full up-elevator and the impact all happened more or less simultaneously.

Our left wheel took the cow in mid-section and just aft of the shoulder; our propeller cut one horn off. This was a full-sized animal. That tough little Stinson picked the four of us plus that cow right up into the air, the cow almost coming into the cabin. She rolled clear over the wing brace-strut, tearing the pilot door and the bottom-of-the-wing inspection covers off. The loggers and I, minus the cow, staggered out over the power lines, air roaring past the missing door opening.

What to do? The left landing gear was obviously badly damaged. There was no aircraft maintenance in our entire County. If we landed and the gear collapsed... the plane would have to be dismantled, trucked and ferried to the mainland for repairs. If we flew the plane to Bellingham (the closest aircraft repair facility) these tired, hungry and thirsty loggers were going to be stuck over there until at least tomorrow, maybe longer (on my tab!). Balls!

I elected to go for a Friday Harbor landing. The gear chattered but did not fail. Dropping off the men, I telephoned Earl Erickson, shop foreman in Bellingham. Earl was aware of my situation; a two airplane outfit; one airplane in the shop for engine overhaul, the other now broken and out of action (with daily scheduled and charter commitments).

Earl said, "Bring it over and we will do the best we can."

The cow impact had come very close to tearing the gear off. To weld the broken fuselage tubing, it required removal of the interior cabin sidewall, floorboards and the exterior fuselage fabric. Earl, with one of his mechanics and myself, worked all night on the plane. At midnight, seeing as how we were all beginning to drag a bit, I drove down to 'The Barrel' (a popular all-night chain drive-in) and bought a sack full of hamburgers and a jug of coffee.

At 7:00 a.m. my Friday Harbor loggers were climbing aboard a Stinson with a big, unfinished silver patch on its side and a pilot with bloodshot eyeballs... but by-cracky, if the Company said it would fly these guys at 7:00 a.m., then that's when we would fly them, right! (thanks to Earl Erickson and his shop).

Junior wasn't too sure... but his partners insisted. The cow was 42 feet from where her tracks dug sidewise into the ground until she hit the ground again on her back. Pat Sandwith, ranch foreman, said that cow was pretty stove-in and sickly for three or four days... looked like she might not make it... then she perked up and was all right.

Except for one thing... that cow was an awful braggart... claimed she was the only Island cow to have ever jumped over the moon! One horn and all!

CHAPTER 20

Island Sky Ferries and a Second Pilot

By the spring of '53 it was obvious that a second, year-around pilot was warranted. Besides... I was about tuckered out. My Ferris employers agreed.

In answer to my Puget Sound queries, Bud Oswald, with his Tacoma flight school, recommended a particularly sharp young man who had just recently finished the commercial course. After meeting with and flying with Bud's recommendation, I hired the young pilot. His name was Bob Fawcett and he was three days younger than I.

I can hardly explain what having a second pilot meant to me. Sure, it meant a welcome division of the workload, but beyond that it filled a need I was only vaguely aware of prior to Bob's arrival. Until then, day after day, through sunshine, fog and storm, I had had no one in the profession to talk to; to compare notes with. Should we go or should we cancel? What do you think of this? What do you think of that? And looking out for each other, one of us would swing by with his airplane just to check on the other; one would land to help the other. And to laugh again... ah that was the best! I'd screw up on something and the three-day younger Fawcett would say, "What can a person expect from an old man?" He'd screw up and I'd say, "Hire a kid and that's what you get!"

Fawcett had only been with us a few days when Captain Ferris hit me with a totally unexpected proposal. He was offering to sell the flying company to me.

The Captain said, or in words to this effect, "Virginia and I have accomplished our goal; that was to help re-establish the airline. It looks like that is now a fact. You have worked long and hard. It is time you were on your own."

Cap wanted to keep two airplanes, the Stinson Station Wagon and the Aeronca trainer. He would sell the Bellingham downtown car and the two Stinson Voyagers to me for what he had in them. He would not charge me anything for the business as he and Virginia considered I had earned it. A handshake and it was done.

I owe those people my eternal gratitude. Now all I had to do was come up with the money.

My Mother had died three years previous. Since then my Dad had been rattling around on the farm by himself, grieving and lonesome. When this chance to buy the flying company presented itself, Dad was ready and willing. He sold the farm and joined Margaret Ann and me in the flying business.

The company we were buying in May of 1953, Island Sky Ferries, Inc. was a corporation. Dad and I split the stock, 50-50. He put up the money. Margaret Ann and I provided the years of experience and skill to make it go.

Our increased passenger and growing freight traffic, plus an increasing demand for mountain and local charter work, made a number of operational changes possible. One of the first things we did was to hire people to drive the downtown Bellingham limo. No more pilots driving the limos. Now when our planes landed at Bellingham, the limo was there waiting for us with outbound freight and passengers. All that was required was a quick transfer. In minutes our inbound passengers were on their way into town and our outbound passengers and freight were "up and away" for the Islands.

With no more driving into town by pilots, I sure did

miss those ice cream floats at the Hillview Dairy that Bob Schoen had introduced me to. They call this progress?

In the meantime, the major challenges facing us were, of course, the condition of the cow pasture that we referred to as an airfield and the fact that our company had no home. That's right, no business office, not even an address. None that is, except my home address. We called an open, unlighted shed and a mud-rutted cow pasture on San Juan Island, home base. Winters of course were the worst, especially during some of our transitional weather of freeze and thaw, freeze and thaw. With wheel fairings off and oversized tires on, with flat-pitched seaplane propellers for maximum power, we wallowed and slid. Takeoffs and landings were made in a sousing bath of dirty water, cow manure and mud.

How crude could you get?

Taking off to the north at King's Field, mud and ruts were routine

I know, I know, it's already been asked, "Why didn't we get on the ball, haul some gravel in, fix up the runway, build a terminal, get lights, etc?

Imagine doing that on someone's private farm. As Lyle King had said, "You can park your planes here on my farm and fly in and out as long as you don't interfere with our farming operation."

No question about it, we desperately needed an airfield with a lighted, hard top runway. An airfield that was reserved for airplanes and people and not for cattle and sheep.

I've had people comment, "Those sound like the fun years." Fun years, my aching back! I had had five years of this mud and cow manure business. Perhaps, I reasoned, the community, after six years of scheduled flight service and several years of medical evacuations, would be ready and willing to participate in the building of a real airport.

So I took my case to the newly formed Friday Harbor Port Commission. I should have asked Dr. Heath to make the presentation for me. The Port Commissioners listened to me and they looked at my rough, hand drawn airport sketches. What one of the Port Commissioners said pretty well summed up their thinking. He said, "We have a seaplane service; why should we, at great public expense, build you an airport?"

He continued, "When I wanted to go into the store business, I didn't expect someone else to build the store for me. If flying is your business and an airport is necessary to your business, then you had better get busy and build one; or choose another profession." The other Commissioners nodded in agreement.

I was shocked. That was it as far as I was concerned. As I arose to leave I said, "Evidently you people are not aware that county governments and port commissions over in America (the mainland) have public airports for the same reason they have public roads."

I should have stayed and argued. I knew that the Commissioner didn't have to finance the construction of the public street to his lot before he built his store... but that's what he was saying I should have to do.

There would be a time, say some 28 years later, when the Port would accept this public airport responsibility. In the meantime, we continued flying medical cases and expectant mothers out of Friday Harbor's unlighted cow pasture; the same at Orcas and Lopez Island.

There were no EMTs (Emergency Medical Technicians) in those days, just one overworked man, Dr. Heath, covering the entire County, day and night. Consequently, the doctor had to ride on every flight, except those times when he was already at a mainland hospital and we flew one of his patients in. That happened every now and then. One time Doc called me from the hospital in the wee hours after I had just gotten home and into bed. He said, "Sorry to bother you, Roy. Can you get over to Lopez Island right away? Mrs. so-and-so is in labor. It's her second child and it will probably go quite fast. There will be car lights out there for you."

So I leaped up, my wife saying, "Good God, now what?"

I dressed, tore out to the airport, flew over to Lopez, picked up the lady and headed for Bellingham. I radioed the airways' people while still 15 minutes out, requesting they call a cab. They didn't acknowledge. All of a sudden the doctor's voice was on the radio asking me how I was doing? It really surprised me. I had never heard anyone's voice on that frequency other than the airways' people.

I answered, "Okay I guess. Lots of groaning; she's got an iron grip on my arm."

Dr. Heath chuckled and said, "Pull in right by the radio

station, I've got a cab waiting."

Later that morning when he was flying home with me, I asked Doc what all that radio and airport cab business was about. He said he took the cab to the airport because he thought there was a good chance the woman would have the baby in the plane.

"Holy Moses, Doc! What if that had happened? What should I have done?"

"If that should ever happen, just cut the cord and tie it off with a string, shoe lace or what have you."

Over the years we had a few close squeaks but thank heavens Doc was always there! I'll say that again, THANK HEAVENS!!

CHAPTER 21

Needed: A New Airport and Ambulance Plane

If, for the sake of argument, I was going to build an airport on this Island, where would I build it? At least that is the way I started to approach the subject. And yet, deep down, I knew if we did not get a dedicated flying field soon, an area free of the ghostly, shifting forms of cattle in the unlighted night with Doc and me engaging in this Russian roulette game—something serious and tragic was going to happen.

So… for the next year, during every spare moment I could find, I was circling and circling with the plane, studying every possible location. Places not suited or appearing to be too expensive to develop were rejected. Those with possibilities warranted further study and a drawn diagram supplemented with an aerial photo, then a ground inspection.

Using known farm-field dimensions (1,320 feet to the side of a square 40-acre field) I was able, from my aerial perch, to judge with reasonable accuracy the size of likely prospects. Considering costs, I studied the lay of the ground—slopes, dips, rock outcroppings, marshes, timber— they all would have a direct bearing on developmental costs.

The ground inspection was difficult. Confirmation of what my aerial observations had suggested required steering a relatively straight line on the proposed runway through brush and brier entanglements, forest, etc. What appeared from the air as a minor mound of rock sometimes was impossible for my budget.

Whew! Maintaining a steady compass course on foot while buried in the forest primeval is not the easiest thing. Especially when I'd hear, far out on the road, my wife laying on the car horn and shouting, "The doctor needs the airplane on Orcas!"

That's right, I was back flying on my own. The entire nation's economy was in a slump. Bob Fawcett had been an auto mechanic for a taxicab company in Tacoma before he came to Friday Harbor. He could now make more money at Walrod's Garage as a mechanic than he could flying for me. So for me, it was back to the seven-day a week bit. As winter set in and the airfields (cow pastures) once again dissolved in quagmires, I became more desperate with each passing day.

The present conditions were literally wearing me and my airplanes down to a nubbin. With every bent propeller or broken wheel our finances became more critical. In desperation I devoted more and more time to the search for that elusive airport site.

Eventually I had four possible sites measured and plotted. The one I liked the best was right on the west edge of town. However, like all the other locations, it had a number of undesirable features. One, it was heavily timbered; two, the only feasible runway layout had both a major rock outcropping and marsh area on it; and three, there was a second marsh in the proposed hangar area. All of those things would of course complicate and increase the cost of construction.

However, I felt the location's many good features outweighed the bad. The best features were: one, being only a short distance inland from Griffin Bay. It was more accessible during low weather flight conditions than the other locations. Second, it was the closest to our traditional Island and mainland destinations by several miles (saving us an estimated 1,100 air and ground miles per month in comparison to the location we were using). Third, it had good approaches for a future runway. Fourth, the land was available. Fifth, considering transient pilots, it was the only location within walking distance of town.

About this time Mother Nature gave us quite a scare. The hangar that Joe Nelson had built for Lyle King and for

Looking south in the early 1950s before Friday Harbor had an airport

Bob Schoen was a three-sided structure open to the west. One winter night my wife and I were having dinner with the Bob Fawcett family when the radio from Victoria, Canada, about 10 miles away, started warning of a destructive west wind that had just struck them. Bob and I exchanged looks across the table; we both knew our hangar was open to the west. WHAM! BAM! An explosion of wind and a shower of broken limbs struck the Fawcett house. Bob and I hit the floor on a dead run. Limbs and treetops were all over the road.

A fearful sight greeted our eyes when our car lights swept across Lynette King-Guard's yard and the hangar area. The hangar was gone. My tethered airplane had pulled one wing stake out of the dirt floor, the other had held. The airplane was lying up on its side, supported by a wing and tail, leaning against two of the structural posts that were still standing. The night was silent and pitch black. Spooky! I had a crawling feeling like out there in the black was a killer watching, waiting to strike again.

No, it was long gone. We don't normally have this sort of thing. I wondered what category this storm would be put into? Thank heavens my old rabbit's foot was still working; the airplane had some superficial damage here and there and one crushed wing tip. No major structural damage! I flew the plane into the Bellingham maintenance shop the next morning.

If that second wing rope had failed the plane would have been part of the debris that scattered across the field and woods for a quarter mile.

That weekend when the cars arrived, I was down on my hands and knees in the grass with a magnet attempting to salvage some of my nuts and bolts that had been on my shop bench. A number of men, including Dr. Heath, walked up and stood looking at me. They didn't say anything. I cautiously stood up and peered back at them… and said, "What?"

A long moment of silence then one said, "Heard you had a little bad luck the other night, thought we'd give you a hand." By that time they were all grinning. One of the men, Roy Gresley, said, "Okay boys, let's gather up all that debris and bring it back here. We'll see how much of it is still usable."

And they did. All those guys, out there dragging boards and metal sheets, Doc Heath and all of them!

Gresley said to me, "Tell me how this building was built." I did. I also told him about working in the hangar during a west wind and the air pressure making my ears pop. "Building was too tight," he said, "That's why she blew away. With an open building you have to let the air flow through."

My Mom used to say, "Things happen for the best." I thought about that. Up until now I had been just about ready to throw in the towel. It seemed as if nobody gave a damn.

Now here were these men. Talk about a boost to a sagging spirit! WOW! By Sunday evening we had a hangar again. Oh it was full of patches and 1,000 old nail holes but it kept the frost and the snow off the airplane and it never blew away.

However... three years later, by the spring of 1956, the year our youngest son, Ken was born, some decisions had to be made. I had just about run my string out. I was still climbing into the back seat of our little four-seat airplane, the doctor lifting while I was reaching out and pulling people in on top of me; people who should have been in a stretcher. The only airplanes we could afford were too small for a stretcher. With no electricity, I was still working on the airplane at night, holding a flashlight in my mouth. Nothing was happening, nothing was getting better. The only thing that was happening was the airplanes and I were getting more beat and dilapidated by the day. It was time either to make our move or get out. I hardly knew my own children. My wife was carrying a tremendous burden.

I'd push the dishes away and lay the head down. "Hush, you kids, you play outdoors now; your Daddy has to sleep." I wanted to quit, and I would have, except for one thing—Dr. Heath. That wonderful man was up and down around the clock week after week, month after month, year after year. We all depended upon him. Hurt? Sick? He would always come with his soft voice, his gentle touch and his caring ways. How can you walk out on someone like that? It just wasn't possible. He needed our airplane. He could not cover this County of islands without it. He had an airplane of his own and he flew, but thank God he didn't push the weather or the darkness.

Dr. Heath with obstetric patient after landing at Bellingham

We needed an ambulance airplane and we needed an airport with facilities. The local County bank couldn't help us with the amounts we needed.

We thought about selling stock in the company. We were advised against it. Ten years prior a local flying company by the name of Island Airways had done just that; had sold a lot of stock to local people and then went broke. One difference, Island Airways sold the stock before they performed; we had been serving the community for almost a decade.

We mailed out a stock offering, $25.00 a share. We said the money would be used for two things—an ambulance plane and an airport for Friday Harbor. The response was amazing, absolutely amazing! Downtown Friday Harbor merchants, resorts, people on Waldron, Blakely, people on Orcas, people on San Juan rallied to the cause. Two children on Waldron Island, the Bucknell boys, took their summer earnings and each bought a share.

And the change of attitude on main street... it was no longer "The Air Service" it was "Our Air Service." WOW!

While our total stock sales came to less than $10,000, the amount was not that important. What was important was what it did to our morale and to our commitment to carry on. Speaking for myself, from that moment on, I never looked back. What a wonderful feeling to know you are not alone and that people recognize and appreciate what you are doing.

Flying Magazine had run an article on a bush type airplane being developed by Wardlow Aircraft Company of Dos Palos, California. It sounded like it was the machine we were looking for. I flew to Oakland to meet Wardlow and get a look at his flying machine. As the airliner let down over Oakland I could see down there on the airport a line of small aircraft parked along a taxiway. One airplane stood out from all the others. I could almost hear that machine talking to me!

Floyd Wardlow, a pleasant, tall man with only one arm, about my age, met me and we went over to look at his airplane. The plane had originally been a 1940 SR-10E gull-winged Stinson 'Reliant'; now modified and remanufactured into an all metal, higher-powered, cargo carrying airplane and renamed 'Bushman."

The original Stinson Reliants were being flown by many northern bush pilots but the airplane had many shortcomings. The main thing was, for its size and weight, it didn't carry that much… and that's what a guy gets paid for, right? The plane was big and stout but the cabin was small, the doors were small and the plane NEEDED HORSEPOWER.

Wardlow dedicated himself to the task.

Unfortunate timing; by the time his conversions were rolling out, DeHavilland of Canada hit the market with their competitive Beaver and even a bigger one, the Otter. Sure, I would have loved to have had a Beaver but the price tag was $45,000.

Wardlow put out five of his popular conversions; I got the last one for $12,500. I was never sorry. In the next 23 years that airplane would save many lives, carry thousands of people, drop food to hungry mountain fire crews, carry hundreds of tons of mail. It paid for itself many, many times over.

Part of the $12,500 deal (a lot of money in the 50s) was that Wardlow would replace the high-time engine with a zero time engine, give the airplane an annual re-license and deliver the plane to me in Friday Harbor within three weeks. He did just that.

At the time I was wondering how a one-armed man could fly an airplane. He was amazing to watch. He'd had almost 20 years of practice; lost the arm in an irrigation pump accident when he was small. Floyd would lean over, tuck the control wheel between the stub of his arm and his chin and do all the throttle, mixture, prop pitch, carb heat, trim tabs, radio, etc. with his one good arm. In the meantime he is taxiing the airplane, steering with his feet, talking to the Tower, looking for traffic, etc. WOW!

I could see this fellow was not going to have any trouble

delivering my airplane to our little Island cow pasture.

Pretty exciting day when that gull-winged Bushman circled Friday Harbor. Floyd made a dandy landing and just about had his one good arm shook off with congratulations. He stayed overnight with us and then I hopped him down in the morning to Seattle to catch an airliner back to California.

Wouldn't you know it? We had a medical evacuation requiring a stretcher that very night. After all those years of night departures, Lynette and family would hardly turn over when the plane went out. That was with the small plane and the 150-hp engine; quite a difference in noise level with the 450 hp Pratt-Whitney. Lynette said she and Frank were sound asleep and when that thing went by not more than 100 feet from their window. Frank jumped straight up in the air taking all the blankets with him and shouted "Good God, what was that?"

CHAPTER 22

Building an Airport the Hard Way

Besides the Bushman in 1953, we purchased the land for our future airport. We bought two pieces; 40 acres from the Mason family and 10 acres of cleared land lying off the south end of the Mason property from Gus Landahl. The purchase of these two pieces of land gave us a total north/south length of 2,300 feet.

As you might imagine, we were running on a lot of promises and mighty scarce on dollars. The weather is what saved our bacon. In 1956 there was a bad fire year in the Mt. Baker National Forest and I had the fire patrol and supply dropping contract. Yes I did! The Bushman and I flew week after week from dawn until dark hauling tons of food and supplies and parachuting them down to the fire crews. That old girl and I paid off those land purchases in one season. How about that! It just goes to show what a person can do with the right piece of equipment.

That 10-acre purchase from Landahl was the jewel. Not only was the property all cleared but in one area it was solid gravel—not sand—gravel! That gravel saved us thousands of dollars. We used it for everything—our road, the runway, the building areas, the taxiway. We used it for the cement floors and the foundations of the shop and terminal, for the turn-up pad and eighteen 10 x 60-foot airplane ramps into the hangars.

I suppose if we had had the money, or the credit, we would have hired a contractor to come in and build an airfield for us. Since we had neither, we had to do it the hard way.

Before anything could be built on our chosen site, a forest had to be removed. Fortunately for us, Roche Harbor Lime and Cement Company, located on the far end of the Island, was still buying second-growth Douglas Fir for their lime-making process.

At the time, property owners were charging one dollar per cord for anyone who wanted to cut wood on their land. We were in a hurry. We advertised "No stumpage-charge on the new airport location." It worked! The ring of the ax and the song of the chainsaw were soon heard from one end of our property to the other. Over 1,600 cords were cut and removed.

By this time, Bob Fawcett (our first pilot) and his family were still living on the Island. Bob was now flying for a Seattle company, a non-scheduled, or non-sched, as they were called in those days. Bob was flying the big twin-engined C-46, Curtis Commando. The company flew personnel charters for the military all over the United States. Eventually Bob's employer sent him to Alaska to sub-contract freight hauling for this country's network of Early Warning radar stations (Dew Line). Bob soon moved his family to Anchorage, Alaska. The Fawcett family settled in and became Alaskans. Some of their children and grandchildren are still there.

In the meantime, I had hired a young pilot out of Bellingham by the name of Herb Vaniman. During the winter of '56, our business was slow (one pilot's worth) so Vaniman did the flying and I did the chain sawing.

Since the new airport property was heavily timbered, my thoughts were of log buildings. I therefore set to work selecting straight and evenly tapered fir trees; falling them, limbing and peeling them and carefully stacking them for curing. They would form the walls of our new passenger terminal and hangars. Ideal conditions existed; the ground was frozen solid and the tree sap was down. These logs were from dormant trees; although it made them harder to peel, they would be fine logs. They would not split when they dried out. By Springtime I had 165 beautiful logs and a year's supply of fuel for my home stove and the Airport Terminal stove.

Old Charlie Carlyle, the carpenter I hired to build the log terminal for us, provided me with some devastating news. According to Charlie, it would cost more to build with logs, even when we owned them, than it would to go out and buy and build with dimensional lumber. Damn! A whole winter's work! As it turned out I should have sought out a second opinion. Charlie knew he was too old and crippled to lift logs. I did not realize that until later. However, I'm not griping. Charlie built us a dandy terminal.

So I had a stack of fine, peeled, seasoned logs on my hands. Fortunately, a Brian Ingoldsby wanted to build a new wing onto his Garrison Bay log home. He bought 150 logs from me for $7.00 apiece. That thousand bucks paid for my winter's wages.

By his financial participation, my Dad had made the purchase of the Air Service possible. Now with the Air Service launching into an airport building project, Dad joined us with even greater enthusiasm. This was something he understood. This was how he and his brother and his Dad had transformed the wilderness into a home and a farm. Every day off and every vacation from his dairy job, he would ride over on the airplane and spend from dawn to dark dynamiting stumps. Pop slept on a cot on our back porch and took his meals with us.

Fred Sundstrom had the biggest bulldozer on the Island. However, it was not big enough to get those stumps out without an individual time-consuming struggle. And then when the dozer did get a stump out, the stump came as a big ball of unburnable roots and dirt.

So we turned to dynamite. By getting a few sticks of dynamite directly under the center of each stump, the explosion would crack the stump and at the same time break off all the little dirt-clinging roots. The dozer could then rip out the stump's four major roots, individually, along with each root's one-fourth of the stump.

What a difference when it came to burning! The dynamited sections burned up cleanly, while whole stumps with their mass of dirt were nearly fireproof. Burning up cleanly was what it was all about. The objective was to create an unobstructed, open flying field. To accomplish this, thousands of tons of forest debris had to disappear. Fire was the only practical answer.

One day this area would be a beautiful sunlit meadow. For now, with the forest gone, it was an ugly, ravaged land. Rough and broken, it lay covered with thousands of tons of rocks, boulders and acre upon acre of fir stumps, limbs and forest debris.

Pop was sitting in the sun, his back to the stump. He was busy loading dynamite 'shots.' I sat down to watch. Cutting off three feet of fuse (burns at a rate of one foot per minute he informed me) Pop crimped an explosive dynamite cap (with his teeth) onto one end of the length of fuse. Taking a stick of dynamite from the box, he made a deep, smooth hole in it with a sharpened stick. Into this hole he inserted the cap-end of the fuse.

"Don't take any chances with possible sparks when around explosives." He said. "Use a wooden spike and your teeth."

With a short piece of string he tied the cap-end of the fuse securely into the stick of dynamite.

Clearing the forest for Friday Harbor Airport

I questioned, "One stick per stump?"

"No," he explained, "One shot per stump--- you can put any number of sticks with it. The shot will set them all off."

Filling a wooden bucket with his prepared "shots," (as he called them), he said, "Come on, I'll show you how to shoot stumps. Bring that steel bar and that case of dynamite with you."

With me grubbing out brush and opening up holes under the stumps with Fred Sundstrom's heavy, man-killing steel bar and with Pop loading and tamping one shot plus two or three sticks under each stump, we eventually had a number ready to shoot.

Pop took the end of each fuse that protruded out of the ground, arched it like the neck of a swan and split the end with his jackknife. "Makes for easier and more positive lighting," he said. Handing me some of those big, wooden kitchen matches, as we used to call them, and two rocks, he said, "You light those two... I'll light these two."

"I don't need two rocks to do that, do I?"

"Put a rock on the top of each of your stumps. After the blasts, if a stump still has its rock, you'll know it's a dangerous hangfire."

"What would you do if we had a hangfire," I asked.

"You ignore it. You go work somewhere else. Tomorrow, when there is no chance of it still smoldering, you come back, dig it out and re-shoot it with a new fuse and cap."

Our flying operations were of course still out at the old King's cow pasture. For the next several years, whenever there was a break in the flying, I was down at our new location either helping Pop, or if he wasn't there, shooting stumps by myself.

It was quite a job. The ground was very rocky. Sometimes, in fact quite often, my burrowing efforts were frustrated by large rocks under the stumps, and I had to abandon a dead-end hole and dig another. In some cases yet another. It was hard work and frustrating. Especially when I would stand up to straighten the aching back and in gazing out across that apparent and endless sea of stumps, realized it had taken me 30 minutes of sweaty effort for just one stump!

It took 10 years to get it all done but when we were finished, our new airport had a lighted, hard-topped, 2,300 foot, north-south runway; a 1,300 foot east-west grass runway for strong crosswinds; a cement floored, heated and lighted 3,600 square foot aircraft maintenance shop; a 15,000 gallon underground fueling facility; 18 aircraft 'T' hangars with cement slab ramps and a car parking area for 30 cars. The airport also had over 2,000 feet of underground tile and culverts for drainage. That was of course the price and sweat we paid for choosing an airport site with marshes.

Our pride and joy was the Terminal. The building

had areas for bookkeeping, reservations, ticketing, and aircraft dispatch with two-way radio communications, four telephones and a heated waiting room with hot coffee and restrooms! We had city water and electrical power. We built our own septic tank and drain field.

Since the building site we chose for the Terminal was on a knoll, we were able to construct the Terminal's cement slab floor and entrance for the convenience of elderly or incapacitated people, to just inches above ground level without worry of water flooding.

Our airport plan and aerial traffic pattern was laid out to take advantage of both the airport's terrain, the neighboring terrain, the town location and the prevailing winds. We built all the airport buildings, fueling facilities, etc. on the north end of the airport, which was the high ground, the town end of the property. This put the building site about 200 feet west of the north end of the main runway.

From here the runway sloped to the south at nearly a two percent grade. Part way up the runway we constructed a high-speed turnoff and taxiway that led straight to the Terminal.

Our temporary terminal on left, with cement slab poured for the new terminal on right

When a loaded airplane left the Terminal for takeoff into our prevailing southerly winds it had only to taxi 200 feet to the runup pad, followed by a most desirable downhill takeoff.

Landings, with southerly winds up to 12 knots, were made towards the Terminal—downwind to the north. Since these landings were made uphill and against the deceleration of the uphill slope, the high-speed turnoff and taxiway functioned perfectly, the plane often rolling up to the Terminal with no brake or further throttle applications required.

Since this meant, as I have described it, takeoffs and landings in opposite directions, the FAA naturally didn't think kindly of it. However, our pilots were all professionals. All of us very carefully broadcast our position and intentions over the radio. In all the years we used the airfield in this manner, I am unaware of a single near-miss occurrence involving any of our company pilots.

However, that was not always true when it came to the increasing number of transient and local pilots who started using our private airfield. While we made it perfectly clear to those who had a radio, there were others, of course, who just blundered in and ended up scaring the hell out of everybody. So the years of zip, zip, zip, had to end. We changed to a conventional flight pattern.

Landing on the crosswind runway

166

CHAPTER 23

Mountain Flying

Since the income from mountain flying is what financed the construction of our new Friday Harbor airport, then maybe I should tell you about that mountain flying.

As you have probably surmised it would be pretty hard to fly 25 summer fire seasons in the high mountains, both in Washington State's Cascade Range and its Olympic Range, without encountering a few situations that would cause one's bottom to bite a few rings out of the seat cushion, right? Well I'm still here, but yes... there were times!

The Bushman dropping supplies in the Olympic Mountains

It was early in the '50s when I got my first introduction to this mountain cargo dropping. The first thing I wanted to do was talk to some of the old fliers who had years of experience doing this sort of thing, who had worked out the methods of dropping cargo chutes and of coping with the high mountain environment. No such luck, they were all gone; old age and the war had done them in.

My ace in the hole was one old ranger, Hubert Wilson. Hubert had been involved and was still involved. He remembered a lot of the details, such as static line length, method of opening the chutes, how many feet the chutes fell before they were fully opened, and... how to make the chutes. I didn't have to worry about making the chutes, however— during the winter, forestry personnel manufactured mounds of burlap chutes.

Another thing that was good, the old Ranger came along on some of my early patrol flights. That really helped me become acquainted with Mt. Baker National Forest's 1,000-plus square miles. Finding a fire that is puffing up a cloud of smoke is one thing, delivering food and equipment to a trail crew that is almost invisible and way, way back in the mountains, that is quite another.

My very first drop assignment was to resupply the fire lookout on Copper Mountain, which is in the northern Cascades and perhaps five miles south of the U.S.-Canadian border. Neither my young "dropper" nor I had had any previous experience at this. The day was beautiful. We were flying a four-seat Stinson Voyager.

For an unobstructed view, lookouts are of course placed on the highest terrain possible. This lookout had a vertical cliff on one side and a steep, rocky slope down on the other.

The first item to be dropped was a five-gallon can of gasoline for the lookout's generator. Considering the tenderness of the heavy, thin-skinned, rectangular can of gasoline, a snow bank near the lookout appeared to be the best landing spot. I made several practice runs; the air was smooth, the run looked good. On our next run, at my count of three, the can was gone; I kicked the tail to the side so we could watch. The chute opened just like they said it would...BULLS EYE! right smack on the snow bank!

As the snow bank slowly changed color, the shouts of elation died in our throats. The can had stopped when it hit the snow bank; the 30 pounds of gasoline had kept right on going. For the next 25 years, the only kinds of five-gallon cans I ever dropped were round ones; they were much stronger.

One of the remaining drop-sacks was quite light; probably bread, mail, blankets or what have you. I was concerned that it might fly back and catch on our tail so I cautioned the dropper to make sure he really shoved down on that sack as it went out the door. He did just as I told him to. The chute went down, snagged on the cabin footstep, opened and immediately started dragging us down. Amazing, the drag of even a small chute! While keeping the plane from stalling by dropping into the open air of the valley, I jerked out my sheath knife and handed it to the dropper. By hanging out the door (with me hanging onto his belt) he was able to slash the riser lines and free the package and the chute.

Obviously, the two of us had a lot to learn.

This particular mountain flight took place during the late 50s, before helicopters had the engine power or perhaps the developed technology to work the high, thin air of the mountains. During this non-helicopter era there were only three ways of getting supplies to fire fighters in the roadless mountain back country; on the backs of men, on the backs of mules, or dropping by parachute from the air.

That is where I came in. I owned one of Floyd Wardlow's modified 1940 Stinson "Reliants." The plane was nearly perfect for the job. Wardlow called his modified gull-winged Stinson, the 'Bushman." It had a 450 horsepower Pratt-Whitney engine on the front end and ten feet of unobstructed cabin aft of the pilot's seat, with two large cargo doors. This gave the plane the power, the capacity and the layout to do the required job.

In later years some of the national forests were combined with others and renamed. During the decades of the 50s, 60s, and 70s when I was flying the mountains, the Mt. Baker National Forest started at the U.S.-Canadian border and ran south, taking in the first 60 miles or so of Washington State's Cascade Range.

This particular summer fire-season was unusually hot and dry; consequently it was plagued with electrical storms and many forest fires started by lightning. It wasn't a surprise then when the forestry fire coordinator called me one evening requesting both the drop plane and a patrol plane for the next day's effort.

So here we were, the Bushman, my pusher, or dropper they called him, and me in the first hour of daylight... climbing steadily upward, lifting our heavy load out of Bellingham towards the waiting mountains. Smoke from yesterday's and last night's lightning-started fires had turned the lower elevation visibility into a hazy murk.

I rubbed the windshield and peered ahead. It looked as though the mountains had considerable cloud cover. To reach our destination we had some high terrain to climb through. I had been hoping for a clear day—at least a higher ceiling.

After eight seasons in the mountains I figured I had served my white-knuckle apprenticeship; had seen it all. Famous last words—this day would prove to be the mother of them all.

Continuing to climb, we left the open country behind

and as we swung into the Nooksack drainage we entered the foothills. Under today's conditions it was like flying into a hangar, the base of the clouds forming the ceiling, rock and timbered mountain walls disappearing up into the clouds on either side.

As we leveled out, just shaving the cloud bases, my altimeter read 5,600 feet. I studied the clouds ahead. Although the bases of the clouds were dark, there appeared to be no roiling action. Good! We wanted nothing to do with any thunderheads.

Getting this flight through on this particular route was most desirable. This was the shortest way to our latest fire and with a full day ahead of us we had no time to spare for detours. This ceiling, however, was going to make it 'iffy.' Ahead were two mountain passes which had to be negotiated before getting to the fire. The first pass was Hannegan Pass at 5,000 feet and the other, Whatcom Pass at 5,200 feet. Held down by a 5,600 foot cloud base, we were going to have precious little space for squeezing through… particularly since those pass elevation measurements had been recorded long ago by someone on the ground and not by someone flying above the treetops.

If getting through proved to be impossible, then we would be forced to backtrack all the way out of the mountains, fly south down Puget Sound to the next county and then fly the roundabout route up the Skagit River drainage. I certainly didn't want to do that—it would more than double our time and mileage to the drop zone.

Yes it's true, as a contractor, time and mileage were the basis of my pay. However right now I wasn't worried about that. With fires and crews all over the Mt. Baker National Forest area and me with the only drop-plane under contract, the big question was where to find enough daylight hours to service them all.

This first flight's destination was a fire on Perry Creek, 50 miles back into the mountains and four miles below the U.S.-Canadian border. The lookout on Desolation Peak had seen the lightning strike last night just at dark. It had all the makings of becoming a bad fire—dry timber and grass, low humidity area and difficult terrain. Smokejumpers out of the Methow Valley jump-base should be dropping on it right about now.

On board our plane we had the jumpers' food, extra tools and clothing, and camp equipment. In fact before the day was out we would be supplying a complete camp for both the jumpers and for the relief ground crew who would very shortly be boating up Ross Lake and then hiking on foot to the fire.

As we approached the Mt. Baker and Mt. Shuksan glacier areas the air stream whipping past the Bushman's open door got downright cold. I was glad I was riding behind our mound of parachute attached supplies instead of next to the open door as the dropper was. Just then the dropper pushed some of the packages over a few inches and shouted at me through the hole. I leaned towards him as far as was possible but couldn't make him out... then he made with his teeth like they are chattering. That I understood. Grinning, I fanned myself as if too hot. I don't think he thought that was very funny.

Flying up the North Fork of the Nooksack River, we branched off into the tight quarters of Ruth Creek, which leads to Hannegan Pass. Now the terrain under us was rising rapidly and the mountain walls on either side were closing tighter and ever tighter. Right at this moment with the pass still around the corner and out of view, I figured our chances of not having to turn back were about 50-50.

Glued tightly against the right-hand canyon wall and skimming the base of the clouds, I slowed the plane and lowered partial flaps. The slower speed would enable us, if necessary, to reverse our course in a minimum amount of space.

We burst around the corner and there at the end of our cloud and rock tunnel, less than a half mile away was the pass—apparently clouded in.

Although we had less than 30 seconds of airtime left, everything seemed to have shifted into slow motion. Fortunately I knew this canyon and I knew my airplane. The brain, without panic or emotion, functions impersonally, foot by foot, calculating and recalculating the dwindling distance and maneuvering room. My hand and foot started the plane into its escape turn while I continued peering at that pass. Suddenly I saw what I had hoped for... just above the treetops I saw a distant rock wall. Throwing the controls hard over, we rolled back out of our turn and popped through the pass.

Good! One more pass to go!

Maintaining our altitude and course, we flew for a few miles across the headwaters of the Chilliwack River drainage... then began threading our way into Whatcom Pass. Although Hannegan Pass and Whatcom Pass are less than ten miles apart and are at almost the same elevation, they are as different as night and day. Instead of a steep little timbered notch like Hannegan, Whatcom Pass is in a world of glaciers, snow, ice, bare rock and gravel...and it squirms around in a curve, up and over the ridge. With 200 feet to spare we cleared Whatcom Pass and are diving down into Little Beaver Creek.

Then we got our first look at the Perry Creek fire. Steep country—fire smoldering in the early morning damp—good sized areas of trees and grass already blackened... smokejumpers' parachutes off to the side, hanging in some low bushes... probably where they will camp.

I called the jumpers on the forestry radio, "Perry Creek Jumpers, this is drop-plane; got some chow for you, over." "Yeah drop-plane," they answered, "We got you... drop it in by the chutes, okay?"

"You bet, here she comes."

As we circled and made a trial run I said, "Breakfast on the next one," then I asked, "Everything okay with you guys, nobody hurt in the jump?" The jumper camp started to answer back when somebody shouted from the background, "Tell that mother to quit messing around and get it on the table!" I laughed and turning, shouted to my dropper, "Looks good... boys are hungry... next pass...on the count of three, okay?"

He nodded and started separating one of the sacks of freight from the pile and attaching the static line to its chute.

As we started our turn to the target I shouted "ONE!" and watched my dropper as he got the sack to the door, checking attachment and clearance of the static line. He read the tag on the sack and shouted, "65 pounds... burlap!"

I nodded and got back to my flying.

We were using two types of parachutes, forestry handmade ones from burlap sacking, and the others, government surplus fragmentation bomb chutes. We used the homemade ones for the heavier loads. They were very reliable but they took awhile to open. The bomb chutes on the other hand were designed to open instantly. For accuracy you dropped the burlap early, giving them time to unwind on their way to the target; we would drop the bomb chutes right over the target.

Checking smoke from the fire for wind drift, I rolled the Bushman out on final approach... throttling back, we eased toward the target.

"TWO!"

With my face pressed against the pilot door window, glancing at the gyro-horizon to make sure the wings are level, I watched the target advance along the nosecowl.

"THREE!"

With a rush of air the package was gone. Leaning out of the open door the dropper watched the opening chute for a moment then swung back in and gave me the thumbs up. Pushing the Bushman to climb power I gained back the altitude lost and reversed course just in time to see our first package hit the ground.

"Right on the money," came the welcome word from the ground. By the time we had unloaded and flown back as far as Whatcom and Hannegan Passes the ceiling had raised a fraction and no longer posed a problem.

That was the first load of the day. Weather conditions remained about the same all morning. In the meantime we hammered back and forth, load after load to this fire and to others, stopping only to refuel and to reload… and to go to the restroom. The airport restaurant was equipped with a two-way radio and at our request kept us supplied with food and drink, which we devoured in flight.

As the day advanced and the sun reached its zenith, things started heating up. By 2 p.m. the air was rough as a cob and the Perry Creek fire was huffing and puffing and threatening to crown. That's when we got into trouble.

It happened about 2:30 or 3 o'clock when we were returning empty; pretty tired, not as aware as I should have been. Suddenly right in front of our nose a geyser-like column of whirling branches and debris came sweeping up off the ground. With a shock I realized the lowering cloud-base directly ahead was no longer smooth but was now rolling like a boiling pot.

We had just committed ourselves to Whatcom Pass's narrow gut. There was no place to go except straight ahead.

With a slam the plane was picked up and spun to the left. With my heart in my mouth I jammed in full opposite controls, knowing full well there was no way we could miss the rock wall. But we did miss it! The upward suction of that huge storm cell must have been our momentary salvation.

Now we were back in the gut; I had the plane standing almost on its nose, the cumulonimbus thunderhead, like a tremendous vacuum cleaner, trying to suck us up.

Talk about frightening! The thought trickled through my nearly numb brain; 'if this suction suddenly turns loose we are going to auger straight into the ground!'

The cloud enveloped us; the only reason I could see was because we were so close to the rocks. We fought over the edge of the pass and down the other side. Without conscious thought, like a drowning person, I clung to the only thing I could see, the treetops. Our airspeed gauge was warning of a dangerously high speed. No time to weigh the odds... a structural failure from the high dive speed or destruction up in the maw of this frighteningly powerful monster; there were no other options.

Suddenly we were in what appeared to be a basin. Slamming the plane around in a tight circle, the windshield smothered with rain, we went around and around, missing tall snags at the last split second, jerking away from timbered walls; desperately looking for a way out.

A tremendously bright flash and a tree right beside our open door took a lightning bolt, instantly bursting into a huge vertical spire of fire. Even our roaring engine noise did not drown out the tremendous clap of thunder.

Jammed into a constant 45 degree banking turn, we continued our blind probing. There appeared to be no way out. One smashing lightning bolt followed another. It seemed as though we were immersed in a deluge of blinding water and an endless hell of fire and noise that would go on forever.

The senses were simply numbed. Flying mechanically, we floundered on. Sometime, probably during the third orbit, a glimmer of hope entered my brain… we just might survive this thing. With that revelation I started to slowly take stock of the situation. I became aware that my hands hurt. No wonder… they were gripping the throttle and control wheel so hard there was no circulation. Keeping the old Bushman in her turn, I cautiously relaxed my grip. My feet! Wonder I didn't break the pedals right off! With the relaxing of the body, things looked ever so much better! All kinds of things flooded into my mind. For years I had flown this forest; always after the fact. What an opportunity to be an on-the-spot eyewitness! To be able to record lightning strikes as they happened!

Record the strikes. To do that accurately I would have to have the dropper's gridded plastic map. I turned and looked at the dropper for the first time since this nightmare had started. He was there in the open doorway, his eyes tightly closed, bent over almost double, both hands locked around the bottom of his seat. I shouted, "Give me the map!" No reaction. I leaned over and shook his shoulder. He was as rigid as a block of stone. I kept shaking him and shouting, "Give me the map!" His lips started to form words but his eyes still remained closed. "Give me the map!" I shouted again. He mumbled something. I gave him a good hard bang on the shoulder and shouted, "What?" With that his eyes flew wide open and he shouted, "Are we lost?"

As I had done only moments before, he slowly came around. Once he understood we were still among the living and realized what needed to be done, he got busy with the map and the grease pencil. Very shortly the rain stopped, the churning of the clouds quieted and began to rise. What a wonderful feeling to be alive and to be able to fly up and down the lovely, wide Chilliwack!

Hannegan Pass was still up in the clouds... but it wouldn't be for long! We tried to contact Copper Mountain lookout on the radio but he was several thousand feet above us and still in the clouds. His radio would still be disconnected and he would be perched up on his glass-legged stool in the middle of the floor of his tiny shack, his heart beating fast and his ears still ringing from the smashing strokes of thunder and lightning that had struck around him.

With time to kill before Hannegan Pass allowed us through, we took the opportunity to prowl. As the rising clouds revealed one after another of the Chilliwack's creeks and tributaries, we toured them recording a total of 18 strikes.

Hannegan opened and we slipped through. Popping out of Ruth Creek and into the Nooksack, we were immediately within radio range of Glacier Ranger Station. My dropper established contact and began feeding them the fire coordinates. When he had finished he gave me a 'thumbs up.' Sliding down in his seat he dropped his map-board on the floor and while the old Bushman hummed her merry tune the two of us just sat there, spent and grinning at each other.

Just about the time we were entering the landing pattern at Bellingham Airport, Copper Mountain lookout came on the air with some hot news for the ranger station. "Go ahead Copper," Glacier said.

Copper started rattling off the coordinates of the many lightning strikes he had observed. Reading back each one for confirmation, Glacier would add, "Thank you, we already had that one."

After being rebuffed for the third time the Copper lookout practically exploded, "How in the blankety-blank hell could you have possibly had these strikes. I'm the only person up here?"

Glacier answered back, "The drop-plane had to circle in your area until the storm was over... he recorded them... didn't you hear his engine?"

There was considerable sputtering and muttering from Copper. I turned to my dropper and asked, "Are you acquainted with the guy on Copper?"

He nodded. "How big is he?" "Pretty good sized," he answered.

After we landed and were taxiing in I said, "You know, that guy has spent all summer up on that lonely lookout just hoping for something to happen that would justify his efforts... then we come along at the crucial moment and steal his thunder. Best he doesn't find out who the drop-plane's crew was, right?"

The dropper rolled his eyes and said, "Right!"

Hope that fellow is no longer in the area when he reads this.

CHAPTER 24

Air Drop in Hell's Canyon

Instead of spring, it felt more like mid-summer. After weeks of warm rains, the skies had cleared. The months that followed, May and June were downright hot. Maybe not Arizona hot but certainly hot for the Pacific Northwest. The first few weeks were wonderful but as the weeks extended into months…people in the tourist business were of course, ecstatic, but those in farming and forestry were beginning to worry.

Our local flying business was buzzing with activity. Survey crews were chartering to and from this island or that; county road crews, telephone and power crews doing the same. Boy, if this weather kept up, the Air Service was going to have a record year! And the schedules! People were just 'up and at em!'

The phone rang… Margaret Ann said to me, "The Forest Service wants to talk to you."

"Forest Service? We don't hear from them until summer."

The man on the line told me that last night the northeastern Oregon and western Idaho area had been hit by a terrific electrical storm; in fact they were still being hit. Seventy-two fires had been reported so far. Our Cascade Mountain area had been spared. Districts such as ours that were unaffected by the storm were rushing crews and equipment to the fire areas.

He said they wanted me to fly the Bushman across

the mountains to the smoke jumper airfield at Winthrop, Washington... pick up a load of cargo parachutes and fly them to the fire coordination center at Baker, Oregon. He warned me to take my shaving gear and some extra clothes along because I would not be released until the crisis was over.

I hated to leave the Islands. We were really busy, but... we had a commitment to a National Forest contract... and... we were all eager to see those Forestry dollars pour into our Friday Harbor airport project. Besides, I knew I had an excellent Island crew and I knew they would turn to and cover all the bases.

Margaret Ann and Roy with their new airplane,
the Bushman, in 1954

When I landed at Winthrop, boy, the load of parachutes they wanted me to carry! I think they were accustomed to loading their twin Beechcraft. When carrying a big load in my Bushman, with its long cabin, I was always careful to load the aft part of the cabin with bulky, light stuff, like sleeping bags and boxes of bread. However, with this load, there was nothing light; those tightly rolled and packed cargo chutes made a pretty solid load.

By the time the Bushman was loaded... from floor to ceiling, from instrument panel to aft bulkhead, there was just enough room left for me to slide through the little pilot door and into the pilot seat. The old girl was sitting right on her aft center of gravity—something a pilot must be careful with.

About the time I was settled and buckled in, several ladies came rushing up with a smallish box. "Can you take this to Baker, Oregon with you?", they asked. "It's not heavy."

"I'm sorry ladies, as you can see I have hardly a square inch to spare." The face on the lady with the box really clouded up... and she softly said, "It's my son's birthday today, he is one of the smoke jumpers down there. I wanted him to have this cake."

I had great respect for those aerial jumpers and I had a pretty good idea, with all the fires, the hazards her son was facing and what this could mean to her. I sucked in my belly and pulled the control wheel back; there were a few inches to spare. With this heavy aft load I knew the control wheel from takeoff to landing would be shoved forward for the next several hours. The lady climbed up on my landing gear wheel and handed the box up to me. I don't think it weighed more than two or three pounds. Pushing the control wheel forward I inserted the box next to my belly, then pulled the wheel back; the box scrunched to about two-thirds of its size. I said, "What do you think? I can do it if you think it is okay."

WOW! Her face lit up in a big beautiful smile and she said, "Heaven thank you! Smoke jumpers are used to things being scrunched."

That birthday cake was a great idea. Instead of having to hold that heavy tail up with forward pressure on the wheel for the next several hours, I could adjust my attitude and speed, up or down, just with my belly!

'HEY LOOK MOM—NO HANDS!"

At Baker, four or five husky young men trotted up to the plane as I shut down. One of the fellas said, "My mother called and said you had something on your plane for me."

As I handed the box to him I said, "You ever hear of pound cake?" He said, "Yeah, but I don't know what it is."

"Well this isn't it," I said, "This is squeezed cake."

"Squeezed cake," he said as he opened the box, "Squeezed cake?"

"When you see your Mom, ask her about squeezed cake."

"Oh, okay," he said, and he and his buddies were gone. Wonder if he ever did ask his Mom?

The Forestry man in Bellingham was right; looks like they had dealt me in. The man running the show at the Baker airport pointed at a spot on the wall map and said to me, "That's where the men from your Glacier district are. They just got in there. They need sleeping bags, shelters and food. Your load is being made up for you right now."

"My load? I had some ideas about finding some chow, a bathroom and fueling my plane."

He grinned, "Right on; there's the bathroom, over there is some coffee and sandwiches, out there is the fueling island. You've got 30 minutes; it will start getting dark in less than two hours."

"Balls afire, why me?"

"When the Glacier boys heard you were coming they passed up a chance with another plane; said they'd rather wait for Franklin."

By this time I was helping myself to a sandwich. "After a compliment like that," I said, "That's when a guy is liable to screw up. How do I find these guys? I don't know this country."

"They are 1,000 feet down on the Oregon side of the Snake River Canyon. There are a lot of fires down there but most of the fires are on the Idaho side. Only two on the Oregon side. Your boys are on the most northerly fire."

"I don't have a dropper."

"We have one for you."

"If it is dark when I get there, any idea on how they will indicate the drop zone?"

"They said you would recognize their signal."

"Really! I hope they're right."

I met the young man who would be my dropper; we fueled the Bushman, loaded her up with a nice, moderate load, rehearsed our drop procedures and then we were ready to go.

A lot of airport activity… one side of the airport was delegated to the multi-engined aircraft and to their loading of the anti-fire liquid solution called borate. I don't remember how many planes were involved in this borate effort but it seemed as though there was one of their planes either taking off or on final approach for landing constantly. Besides that, there were patrol and drop planes buzzing everywhere. We sandwiched in between airplanes and departed in the evening twilight for Hell's Canyon. With Sacajawea Peak on the left, we flew northeastward.

That Snake River canyon, called Hell's Canyon, is really something; deeper than the Grand Canyon, some say.

River runs south to north in that area. Our fire, on the West Bank of the canyon, the Oregon side, was almost obscured by smoke and deep shadows. No problem with the terrain, the canyon was sufficiently wide for our type of maneuvers, providing of course it didn't get so dark that we couldn't see it. The thing that concerned me was that it was getting darker by the minute and with no radio communications or even tents to spot, there were nothing to indicate where the men were and where we should drop our load.

The crew had told the man, "Franklin will recognize our signal." Balls, what signal?

The fire was on the steep canyon wall. Below the fire was a ledge area of an acre or so, probably where they would camp. We made a slow, low pass over the ledge area. BY GOD! Beautiful! A circle of flashlights glowing up at us! What a deal!

Sooo, how were we going to do this? If they stayed in the circle and we dropped something heavy… and if the chute should stream… in the dark they wouldn't see it coming and somebody could get seriously hurt or killed. We decided to drop the big ball of sleeping bags first. It had no chute but it was light and soft. On the count of three we kicked the sleeping bag bundle out early, making sure it would not bounce past and over the cliff.

Suddenly there were only four flashlights left. Guys were still laughing about it a month later. Said they heard the thing swat the ground and the next thing they knew the thing mowed them down like a big, soft bowling ball, STRIKE!

Anyway, they knew we had the range and didn't need their lights anymore. They got off to the side and out of danger while we unloaded the rest of their cargo. No chutes failed and everything came in okay. The dropper and I headed back to Baker for food and sleep. For the next ten days we would be loading the Bushman and heading out, from dawn until dusk, with food and supplies for crews working on many fires.

At the beginning of this chapter I made a point of mentioning the warm rains of an early spring and then the high temperatures the Northwest was receiving. I was told these conditions caused an unusually tall growth of early grass in the beautiful, high parklands of eastern Oregon and western Idaho (great elk country). Then the hot months turned the grass into dry tinder.

When the lightning struck those thousands and thousands of acres of grass and stands of Lodge Pole Pine, they burst into flames. Within the first 24 hours, at least in the John Day area of Oregon, dozens of those individual fires had run together into one tremendous conflagration. Men with bulldozers had been dispatched and had begun to scrape out firebreaks; now suddenly they were cut off and trapped.

Here came the Borate Bombers! The bombers started with the men and machinery; painting a path for them, right out through the flames and to safety.

I thought that was really cool!

Eventually I got home. My pilots crowding around, speculation running wild. "You were certainly gone long enough. Did you make enough to finish building the maintenance shop?" And then of course, some good natured, "I'll bet all the time we've been down here flying our butts off, he's been up there fishing those mountain lakes."

We finished out our maintenance shop… A dream come true!

188

CHAPTER 25

Flying the President

Mr. Bill Allen, President of Boeing Aircraft Company, reminded me of my Dad. Both he and my Dad stood about five foot nine, had a moderate build, wore glasses and a pleasant expression and were probably about the same age. They both had a twinkle in their eyes.

How did I get acquainted with the President of the Boeing Aircraft Company? Miracle of miracles, he booked on our Seattle to Orcas Island flight. Can you imagine? We were flying a summer schedule with single-engined landplanes over the timber, water and farms of Puget Sound and this man who probably had access to just about any type of flying machine known to man booked with us.

On that particular day I was flying the Seattle schedule. In those days we went in and out of Boeing Field and not Seattle-Tacoma International. On this flight I had two passengers booked to Seattle and a Mr. Allen booked on the return flight to Orcas Island. Since there was a family of Allen's on Orcas, I assumed my return passenger was one of them. I had not the slightest inkling I was about to meet Boeing's headman.

As I taxied up to the Boeing Field terminal I thought I recognized a man who was standing, watching us from the other side of the fence. He sure looked familiar. Newspaper pictures… that was it! That's who he was. Mr. Allen, president of the Boeing Aircraft Company. A few seconds later it hit me; we had a Mr. Allen booked on our next flight. No way! The president of Boeing would not be travelling in a little single-engined airplane. And yet… this Mr. Allen had a suitcase with him and he was definitely interested in what I was doing. With a rapidly increasing pulse I began to realize Boeing's Mr. Allen was my 'Mr. Allen.'

Trying not to trip over my own feet I stopped in front of this man, set my passenger's luggage down, stuck out my hand and said, "Mr. Allen, I understand you are flying with us to Orcas Island." His handshake was firm and he looked me right in the eye as he said, "Yes, I'm booked on your flight 721…" (we used big flight numbers to make it sound like a big outfit). "Is this our airplane," Mr. Allen asked? I gulped and said, "Yes sir, we will be departing in just a few minutes." And so we did.

Naturally, along with everything else, the ceiling was only about 1,500 feet. Thus, instead of cruising at a good comfortable altitude, we were down at 1,000 feet flying up the middle of the shipping channel. Mr. Allen, my one and only passenger, was perhaps having some second thoughts for he was sitting forward on his seat, grasping the windshield brace and peering out over our one and only engine.

Suddenly he turned to me and demanded, "What would you do if you had an engine failure at this very moment?" Whenever a pilot is flying a single engined landplane low and over this sort of water/timber terrain the possibility of an engine failure is always under consideration. In this case I knew exactly what I would do. I answered, "Good time of year for it."

Silently he turned back to his forward vigil. In ten seconds or less he whirled and barked, "Why?" "This month, the month of June, has some of the lowest daytime tides of the year," I answered. "See those people down there? They are digging clams on beaches that are seldom exposed. If you and I had an engine failure we could glide into any one of those beaches.

Mr. Allen turned and studied the beaches for a minute or so then turned back to me and asked, "Wouldn't those tide flats be pretty soft?" "Yes sir," I replied, "Some would certainly be soft; might even cause the plane to flip over. The important thing however... you and I would walk away from it."

Evidently I passed muster for it wasn't too long before Mr. Allen was sitting back, relaxed, and telling me about one of his early aviation adventures. An opportunity to converse with one of the aviation pioneers is a rare privilege. I hope you agree with me because I am about to repeat Mr. Allen's story, okay?

Mr. Allen was crossing Wyoming's high country as the only passenger in an open cockpit, bi-winged mailplane. It was Fall and an early snowstorm caught them. Fortunately they spotted through the swirling snow a cattle ranch and were successful in landing near the ranch buildings.

The storm did not let up until the third day. On the second day the rancher handed each of his two guests a shotgun, along with a blanket and said, "About time you boys earned your keep." Bending over under the blanket (making like a cow going to water) the two were able to approach their quarry undetected. BLAM! BLAM! Mr. Allen said the roast Canadian Honkers were sure good.

For the remainder of the month of June, Mr. and Mrs. Allen traded houses with an Orcas Island couple. The Orcas people moved to the Allen house in the city, the Allen's to the Island; commuting back and forth with us as required.

In those days our company's San Juan County service area consisted of ten scattered, thinly populated Island communities (the total County population, before the Islands were discovered in the 60s was less than 4,000). Traffic on our Seattle schedule was therefore very marginal.

Operationally, passengers from and to the scattered communities were funneled through our home base, Friday Harbor. From there the flights to and from Seattle were non-stop.

During this multi-daily Friday Harbor passenger transfer, Mr. Allen very seldom came inside our little terminal. Instead he stayed outside observing with obvious keen interest the speedy comings and goings of our little puddle-jumper shuttle service.

During one of these 'quickie' transfers, Mr. Allen asked me if any of our routes were subsidized. "No sir," I said, "Not a single mile, but I'm sure considering it."

"Don't do it," he said, "Regulation would ruin this wonderful little local service of yours."

One June day I was flying our '747' on the Seattle to Islands run (the plane we referred to as our 747 was our biggest airplane of the moment, a six-place Wardlow modified Stinson Gull-Wing... now called 'Bushman.') On this flight I had four northbound passengers on board; one for Shaw Island, three for Orcas Island. The three for Orcas were Boeing's Mr. Allen and two of his son-in-law executives.

I had a problem. My radioed instructions from dispatch were to bypass Friday Harbor; go direct to Shaw, then to Orcas. As soon as I was unloaded at Orcas there would be five passengers for me to fly to Bellingham. At Bellingham there would be both passengers and freight to bring out on the 5 p.m. schedule. Our flight scheduling was made deliberately tight. That way our schedules to and from Seattle (which was to the south of our Islands) and the Bellingham schedules (to the north of us) could dovetail and compliment each other as they picked up and delivered passengers. This way we got a high utilization out of our aircraft and none of our customers had to stand around for very long waiting on our flights.

That was all well and good but my problem at the moment was the airport at Shaw. I had already been told by one company CEO that Shaw was more thrill than he was bargaining for. I did not want to lose the Allen account or friendship. However, if I overflew Shaw and took the Allen people direct to Orcas (which is what I would like to do) then come back to Shaw with my one passenger, then back again to Orcas for my Bellingham load, I would foul up the whole afternoon's time schedule. It was a tough decision but I finally decided I would fly the schedule as it was published… Shaw first.

Let me tell you about this Shaw Island Airport. All early airstrips in the Islands were private. Uncle Sam didn't have a dime invested in any of them. These strips usually consisted of some local aviation enthusiast's mark across a back pasture.

Shaw's airstrip was a lot more elaborate and exciting than that. It was masterminded, financed, constructed and owned by a local ex-GI and aviation enthusiast named Wayne Fowler.

The property Wayne owned was heavily timbered and more or less straight up and down; but that didn't stop him. Wayne constructed his airstrip in the only place he could; right through the timber and up the side of the mountain. The strip was very short and very steep, to say the least.

The unbelievable part of all this— a County road with its power and telephone lines went right smack across the middle of Wayne's runway! That's right, the County road popped out of the timber, crossed the runway and disappeared into the timber on the other side. Wayne Fowler later re-routed the road so that it no longer crossed the runway.

If there was no howling wind, landing or taking off from this strip (once you had the hang of it) was not all that bad. For landing you simply dropped down into the narrow approach slash in the timber, picked the nose up with power and landed on the uphill slope. You certainly didn't need any brakes; in fact once you crossed the road you really had to pour it on to get to the top of the strip. There at the top you turned sidewise (so the plane didn't leave without you), shut the engine off, locked the brakes, unloaded or loaded your passengers, cranked up, turned and came screaming down the hill on takeoff; the short, steep grade giving you the speed required for flight.

The tricky part was, this hillside piece of runway was not long enough to allow you to fly out over the utility wires, consequently you had to hold your wheels tight to the ground as you came down the hill, scoot under the wires, cross the road and then rotate. (If you need to use a burp sack they're in the map slot next to your knee).

So here we were. All through the landing, the hill climb, the shut down, the unloading of the passenger, the startup, the down hill drop, the road and wires, the howl up through the timber… not a word, not a sound came from my Orcas passengers.

I rolled out on a course for Orcas, dreading what would be said when we got there. We landed. Mrs. Allen and daughters were waiting for their husbands. As I handed Mr. Allen his suitcase he said, "Give me a minute, Roy, I want to talk to you." He went over to the car, kissed his wife, stowed his suitcase, turned and came back to me; no smile, just his steady, solemn gaze. I was sure I knew what he was going to say, 'under the circumstances, Roy, my people and I will not be riding with you any more.'

Mr. Allen asked, "How often do you go into Shaw Island?" I gulped and said, "Passenger wise, hardly once a week." "How much do you charge?" "Same fare as the other Islands." "And it is on your schedule? You will go in there for one fare?" "Yes sir." "If I paid you a passenger fare, would you go in and out of there?" "If you asked me to, yes sir."

"Here's what I want you to do," Mr. Allen said, "Every time any of my Boeing people are on your airplane I want you to go in and out of that Shaw Island airstrip and then send me the bill." Seeing the question in my eyes he said, "Roy, I want my people to experience real grassroots aviation."

The next time Boeing engineers flew with us they cornered me with a question, "Do we have to land on Shaw Island?" "No," I said, "Not today, this wind makes it too tricky." "Whew! Thank heavens!" was their relieved comment.

It was a privilege to know the revered President of the Boeing Aircraft Company. We will never forget Mr. Bill Allen, his family and those Island flying days of yore.

CHAPTER 26

Night Flying

Did I ever tell you about our pilot, Bill Booze, and Lopez Island's automatic runway lights? I can just hear you say, "No, but I have a feeling I'm going to hear about it." Right? Right.

This little adventure took place on a Sunday evening during late summer. During this particular era our Seattle/ Island clientele, determined to capture every last moment of the waning summer weekends, consistently booked our late Sunday evening Seattle flights to capacity.

At our northern latitude and in late summer, daylight shortens up very rapidly, so we had to make sure our customers were gathered up from the various unlighted island airstrips and on their way before dark set in. As long as the weather held, it wasn't any big deal for our empty 'planes' to return after dark to the home Island.

That's right, 'planes' plural. We're not talking about an airline where everybody waves goodbye, the plane thunders down the runway and everybody climbs into their cars and goes home. Nope, we are talking about our little 'Tunerville Trolley airline' (before we owned any of the higher capacity multi-engined airplanes). At this stage of the game it was four pilots and four loaded single-engined airplanes departing southbound just before dark; later, four empty airplanes returning.

So here we were, the four of us in Seattle, our passengers delivered. It is dark; we are hungry, tired and ready to fly home except for one little problem. An Islander is at our Seattle counter wanting a ride home to Lopez Island.

So…? Isn't that what we're in business for?

"Yeah, right… but Lopez airport has no lights and the moon will not be up for hours! Besides that, the strip is buried in an uninhabited forest area and no one is expecting this guy. That means there will be no car lights, no house or yard lights, no nothing to help identify the airport location."

Bill Booze, flying one of our new Cessnas, was confident he could pick up the clearing with his new, super-bright landing lights. He took on the Lopez passenger and we all departed for home. I was flying our biggest airplane, the Stinson Bushman. Like Booze, Nichols and Palmer were flying Cessnas.

Thirty-five minutes into the flight, Booze started making his letdown for Lopez Island; the other planes continued on for home.

It was mighty dark; the airport-end of Lopez Island was just a black blob against the slightly less black of the surrounding sea. I was concerned for Bill; not that he wasn't an excellent pilot but it had been a long day and I knew he was tired.

I had done plenty of that kicking the nose left and right, playing landing lights back and forth over the forest tops, attempting to spot a clearing in time to land. Then when you do see it, darn! You're off to the side and just missed it! So you go around and try again. If you have no landmarks or light to steer by, it is often again and again. It is wearing, and if you are tired, you are playing a form of Russian roulette.

So I am working on a plan. I have never tried it before… not even sure it will work… should be no harm in trying, however. The thing was, my plane was equipped with two tremendous, nine-inch retractable seal-beam landing lights. When those babies came on they really lighted up the countryside.

My plan was to be several thousand feet above Bill and then at the right moment I would glide down with my lights shining on the airport area ahead of him. Figured as long as I was above him there would be no chance of blinding him with my lights, and... although I would lose sight of Bill during my glide, there should be no danger of collision if I remained above 1,000 feet. So I got into position, lights cycled into the down position and turned off, engine throttled back, flaps extended. Kicking rudder and skidding my plane slightly sidewise I peered down into the blackness below. Where the heck was he? There he was! Way down there! The little finger of Bill's landing lights probing this way and that across the treetops. Over I went, engine at idle, lights blazing. Sure enough, by flattening out just a trifle, my lights were right on the Lopez airstrip clearing...

Bill's announcement on the radio, "Two Zero Yankee on the ground at Lopez" came just moments before I leveled out at 1,000 feet.

Great!!! I turned for home. No conversation that night; just rapid work as the boys put their planes to bed and then helped me strip out the Bushman seats in preparation for the morning mail run; or a night evacuation callout.

Then it was to home and to family for all of us.

During a coffee break the next day, Bill Booze divulged some exciting news, followed by a question. "Lopez Airport has landing lights!" "They're a heck-of-a lot better than ours—if Lopez can have lights like that, why can't we?"

Wow! All of us pilots had been taking our turn covering night medical evacuations and every unlighted airstrip had been a constant sweat case. Lopez Island was the third largest island in the Archipelago with the third largest population. We were all excited over the news!

In rapid succession Bill was asked, "How many lights? Are they on both sides of the runway? Are they the full length of the runway? Is there a lighted windsock?"

Bill scratched his head, "No, it's more a floodlight system. Must be light activated because they came on when I was shining my landing lights in that direction... but then they went off just after I touched down and made my radio announcement. So maybe they're also radio activated?... But then when I tried to turn them on for takeoff, nothing happened. I razzed the engine several times, flashed the lights, triggered the mike button but still they wouldn't come on. Shucks, I don't know... I'll tell you this though; they sure lit up that airfield! Just like day!"

We were all disappointed; me worse than any of them when I realized Lopez had no lights other than the Bushman and me. Bill could hardly believe the old Bushman lights were that powerful.

The idea of two airplanes (and pilots) responding to unlighted airfield night emergency calls (one ambulance plane, one plane to light the landing area) was considered and rejected. We were all young men and eager to serve our communities but there were just so many dollars in the kitty and so many hours in the day and in the night... and no more.

Well there you are: the story of Billy Booze and the mysterious night illumination of Lopez Island's airport. Lopez eventually got a hard-top runway and a conventional lighting system, along with a lovely rotating beacon like a bookmarker, to mark the place.

Our night operations on other Island airstrips were all challenging. In the early years at King's cow pasture, I mounted reflectors along both sides of the runway. With my landing light that helped quite a bit. On many occasions, either there or at other airstrips without reflectors, I would use the "three-car approach." I would ask that one car park at the approach end of the "runway" with its lights shining up the strip, a second parked midway up the strip with its lights across the strip and the third at the end of the strip with its red tail lights marking the far end. This method worked quite well, but every night landing got our full attention.

CHAPTER 27

Operation Seawall

During September of 1961 the U.S. military decided to use our Island as the site for a joint military exercise. The exercise would be called "Operation Seawall."

Several months before this all began, a man dressed in civilian clothes and flying a small single-engined plane, landed at our airport. The man was very friendly, said he was with the U.S. Military and was here to make preliminary arrangements for Operation Seawall.

According to him, the coming operation would be a joint effort involving an invasion force (the Red Army) who would occupy the Island and then the good guys (the Blue Army) would come storming in and save us all. The whole thing would take about ten days. He said the invaders, the Red Army, would like to base a 200-man helicopter operation on our airport.

Well now... fraternizing with the Red Army? I was not too sure about that. Oh, he assured me the military would not interfere with our daily civilian operation... and if I played my cards right there could be some nice change earned through gas sales.

Hmmm.. now that was a bit different!

All the Army would need from us would be lots of space and plenty of high-octane fuel. Oh Momma me! We makah dah money!

This visiting coordinator and I discussed our airport and various ideas as to where to put this 200-man camp. No question about it, our beautifully grassed and green 1,300-foot crosswind runway would be ideal. All I would have to do was close the crosswind runway to everyone except the military. No problem, Great! Perfect!

However, fuel was something else again. The big problem was that neither of the two oil companies serving the island, Standard and Union, had a dedicated storage tank on the Island for aircraft fuel. Standard was considering the possibilities... but it would cost a lot of money and the projected annual return appeared to be very marginal.

The only way we were getting aircraft fuel to our Island airport at this moment was through Standard and through a most difficult procedure. Fifty-five gallon drums of fuel were being transported as deck loads on Island-bound fuel barges. This method required a lot of back breaking hand labor. Our local Standard agent had to unload those drums from the barge, load them onto a truck, and deliver them to us at the airport. We then had to manually empty each drum of fuel into our underground fuel storage tank.

Just for our company use alone it was bad enough, but man! To consider handling thousands of additional gallons for the military? However... except for the inconvenience of the barrels, we actually did have the installation required. When we built our airport's fueling island we had installed two underground tanks and pumpers, one to serve our present 80 octane, small airplane requirements, the other to take care of future, larger aircraft and their higher octane requirements.

So why not? Maybe it would cause Standard Oil to put in that much needed waterfront storage tank. I ordered 36 barrels of fuel (1,980 gallons).

The gas company delivered the last of the barrels and departed with my check just two days before the Army was to arrive. In the meantime Pappy and the boys and I had been busy dumping the barrels of fuel into our empty underground storage tank.

And then here came the Army! Trucks and more trucks, men everywhere, equipment, jeeps, tents, cook stoves!

Then the helicopters started arriving... and very shortly their tank-trucks loaded with fuel arrived. They had their own fuel? I couldn't believe it! The next day the General arrived in his helicopter. It was a hot day; we had the doors and windows of our passenger-terminal/company-office/dispatch center wide open for ventilation.

The General did not land down by his camp, which was only a 100 yards away. No he did not; he landed right smack in front of our little terminal! The wash of his rotors shredded the blossoms from my Dad's carefully manicured and much admired beds of flowers! The rush of dirt and air into our building scattered paperwork everywhere; our barometer was swept from the dispatch wall and sent smashing to the floor!

The General dismounted and strode into our disheveled headquarters. Glancing around at the dirty and obviously unkempt interior (and at me on my knees trying to salvage what was left of the barometer), the General then drew himself up into his academy, ramrod straight posture and announced in a strong and commanding voice, "As of now, all civilian air activity on this field will cease until the present military exercise has been completed."

I'm not kidding you... I remember the General's face but I do not remember exactly what I said. It must have been pretty good because sometime after the General had departed and the dust had settled, our daughter, Susan, came out from her bookkeeping department and gently remarked, "I'll bet that General won't ever forget Friday Harbor!"

Apparently my ' off the cuff' remarks were effective, for neither the General's helicopter nor any other helicopter ever landed in front of our terminal again, and…both our flight operations and the Army's operations functioned throughout the duration of 'Operation Seawall' with no apparent interference.

Concerning our 1,980 gallons of high-octane fuel that we had purchased for the Army? Yes, I remember that subject as being included in my remarks. Although I had no name, no authorized contract, no nothing… and as the General said, "The Army could buy fuel for less than my purchase price," nevertheless the General agreed to purchase our fuel for exactly what we paid for it.

That's not the way to make money but it wasn't a bad deal when you consider the stupid error I had made. I should have known the 'scout' for the Army who sold me on the possibility of gas sales was either blowing smoke or didn't have his facts put together. Anybody should have known the military would not consider activating an exercise that depended upon the availability of fuel from a local service station that was in the contested area (the Germans, out of necessity tried that during the 'Battle of the Bulge,' and they failed).

So it was a relief to recover our investment from all this useless fuel, even if it did cost us some hard work. As my Mother would say, "Valuable experience does not come cheap."

You know… as time went on, we all got kind of used to these 'Red Army' guys. One African-American officer with a big grin came up the hundred yards from their camp to our little terminal and challenged me to a game of ping pong. He was a nice guy. He was still grinning when he left although I had waxed him good.

The word was out; a coordinated aerial, amphibious rescue assault by 'Blue Army' forces was set for daybreak tomorrow morning. They would storm ashore from the

Straits of Juan De Fuca and onto our west beach area. There would be thousands of troops, landing craft, tanks, assault helicopters, fighter jets.

Fellow flyer Wayne Fowler from Shaw Island and I were discussing the situation. It didn't seem fair. Blue Army had jets and all kinds of stuff. All the Red Army had was some troops, tanks and helicopters.

Ah, the dawning of a neat idea! Wayne had a WW-II fighter aircraft; a Navy Grumman F6F Hellcat stashed away in the woods on Shaw. He suggested cranking that baby up and giving the morning's assault force at least a taste of resistance.

Got me all excited!! Trouble was…the Army would instantly recognize any of my aircraft.

A day or so later, the General paid me a visit. He wanted to know if I knew of someone on this Island who had an old trainer plane? Thank heavens he said, 'this Island' and 'trainer plane.' I could honestly say, "no sir, I do not." (Shaw Island was certainly not this Island and that F6F was not a trainer!)

"Well," the General said, "This old trainer, going like the hubs of hell, went right through our coordinated attack the other morning. It was a reckless, irresponsible thing to do and could have caused some serious problems."

I tried to keep from grinning. I said, "Interesting isn't it, General; reckless and irresponsible on the one hand, heroic on the other. Maybe some day the 'Red Army' will find that guy and give him a medal."

The General growled deep down in his throat and departed.

The Red Army lost that day but they would never forget the propeller job that came out of the morning sun, screaming wide open and going like the hubs of hell!

YAHOO! I salute the Shaw Island Air Force!

CHAPTER 28

A Divine Intervention?

This flying that I was doing out in the Islands... I would run into different things, situations that would almost defy imagination. For example, the following experience that I wrote about many years ago still astounds me.

The dreary winter dragged on. For some people the penetrating chill of the continuing southeasters and the cold rain could be mighty depressing. Who could say— maybe the weather had nothing to do with it? One way or another, the young woman in the stretcher had very nearly ended it all.

The young Orcas Island doctor, bracing himself against the howling wind, shouted, "I prefer Anacortes but if there is a question of safety, anywhere will do." I hesitated for just a moment. Every local pilot knows that during a southeast gale, Anacortes's single southwest runway can be a treacherous handful. Under these circumstances air currents spill down from high wooded hills and form a vicious, twisting crosswind.

We had very little choice; the patient was critical and Anacortes had the closest hospital. As we climbed out of Orcas Island for Anacortes it was obvious that the young woman was slipping away. Not that I could tell but when a doctor rips off his safety belt in heavy turbulence and really gets rough with a patient, you know the situation is desperate.

It's times like this when two miles a minute seems

like a snail's pace, and yet, we simply could not push faster in this turbulence without risking the airplane and all of our lives. Climbing steeply, I sought smoother air aloft. At 2,500 feet we were above most of the ground turbulence and could now push the plane to the maximum. Over Blakely Island and facing the open waters of Rosario Strait, I lowered the nose and started the final dash for Anacortes.

Slowly the young doctor returned to his seat, his face covered with sweat and twisted with anguish. The young woman was gone.

I wondered if there were many people out there who realize what these dedicated medical people go through. Slowing the airplane, we continued in silence. Suddenly we were hit by a solitary, breathless drop. The unstrapped body of the girl, the doctor's bag and everything else that wasn't tied down, flew up to the ceiling only to smash back down a moment later.

Hurriedly the doctor restrapped the body… and in so doing a strange look came over his face. Stethoscope in ears, he listened intently and a great shout burst from him, "Her heart is beating! She's with us again!"

On the flight back to Orcas the doctor and I flew in silence, as if in a dream… each of us immersed in our own private thoughts. Far to the west, beautiful sunbeams, the first in many days, were pouring down through breaks in the overcast. The storm was finally passing.

PS— This flight took place during a time of heavy flight activity and the subsequent complications caused by a series of storms, during which I understand the Orcas doctor left the area. Unfortunately, I have no knowledge of who this girl was, why she attempted to take her own life or what she did with the life that was given back to her. I hope she made good use of it and lived a long and happy life.

CHAPTER 29

Some Family Stories

I suppose everyone has a special family adventure they chuckle about. Here's one that my family has chuckled over for many years. I call this story,

"The Island Guide"

By this time you are probably more than familiar with the situation— Margaret Ann and I working straight through the summer in a scramble to earn and store enough chestnuts for winter survival, etc. So right smack in the middle of this grind, my brother Glenn shows up on vacation. Glenn's wife, Jean, had elected to use her part of their vacation for a trip back to her homeland, Scotland. In the meantime, Glenn came to the Island to visit us.

Although Margaret Ann and I were happy to see him, we had just about enough time, per day, to say Hi, and that was all. If he had been a pilot I would have put him to work. Our unemployed eight-year-old son, Ken, saved the day. Ken and my brother became the inseparable fishermen.

Years later the family was still chuckling over one of their summer adventures. One day the two of them were fishing from our open, outboard powered skiff (sans compass) in the area we call the 'outside,' the side of our Island that faces the Strait of Juan de Fuca.

My brother had a salmon on. Totally absorbed in the battle, neither fisherman noticed the incoming fog. By the time the salmon was brought to gaff, the fog had blotted out everything. Belatedly cranking up the motor, they started poking through the vapors that surrounded them. Sitting in the bow clutching his shimmering silver prize, my brother peered apprehensively into the fog. He knew he was completely turned around and lost. He also knew one course would take them to safety, the other to 30 miles of open, fog-shrouded sea. But which way... which way was the right way?

One thing for sure, he thanked God for this confident young Islander at the tiller. Turning in his seat to better admire this intrepid guide of his, the sight that greeted his eyes almost caused him to swallow his Adam's apple. Holding the motor's tiller in the crook of his leg, the boy, using both hands, had the front of his sweatshirt stretched out as he tried to read the promotional area map printed on its surface! Yes... by the luck of the draw, the two of them bumped into a familiar shoreline and eventually followed it home.

Of course in later years 'the guide,' now a trans-Pacific jet pilot for Fed Ex would claim to have had the combined skills of Davy Crockett and Daniel Boone! Just between you and me... I'll bet under that uniform he is still wearing a sweatshirt with a map on it.

I call this next little flying adventure,

"Piece of Cake"

I was flying the afternoon Islands/Bellingham schedule. Just as I was preparing to leave Friday Harbor, dispatcher Margaret Ann received a frantic telephone call from the local Eastern Star Organization. Seems they were having an important function that evening and had just discovered that a cake, vital to their ceremony, had not made the one and only afternoon ferry. Could we possibly bring it out on our flight schedule? With just freight and no passengers and visualizing a lap-size cake, I said, "Sure."

Well... it wasn't lap-size; in fact its container box was

so big I could not begin to get it through the airplane door. What to do? I sliced open the box. The cake only took up a fraction of the box's capacity. The cake was in the shape of a cross; about two or three inches deep, perhaps 18 inches wide and 3 feet long. It was mounted on a piece of stiff cardboard backing.

I picked the cake up, careful to keep it level, and using the only area in my little airplane that was long enough, I suspended the cake between the top of the co-pilot's seat and the top of the back seat. The cardboard backing appeared to be adequately strong.

By the time I had climbed out of Bellingham, flown to Orcas and landed with no apparent objections from the cake, I had become pretty relaxed and self-confident. After unloading my Orcas freight I departed for Friday Harbor. While still in the climb I casually glanced over at the cake and was horrified to see the cake sliding backward and slowly folding up as it squished against the rear cabin upholstery.

Jerking my seat belt off I turned around and kneeling on the seat, I reached under the cardboard backing and raising the aft end up I slid the cake back to its original position; or I should say I was in the middle of this balancing act when suddenly my side window and windshield was filled with seaplane.

It happened so suddenly — a silver seaplane standing on its nose, desperately trying to avoid a collision. Good Lord, it was there and gone in a flash. I was kneeling, with an open mouth and an armload of cake. What a ridiculous way to die!

I felt terrible that my inattention had nearly caused a fatal mid-air collision. After the enthusiastic Eastern Star girls had left with their cake and the assurance that damage to it was negligible, I put my plane to bed and went in and

214

called the Lake Whatcom seaplane base. Even in that flash I had recognized Les Bergsma's little silver Cessna 140. I hated to make this call. Les and I were not the best of friends. I expected to really get reamed out.

Les came on the line, all apologies. Said he was letting his 12-year-old son fly the plane. When the boy shouted, "Dad...DAD!" Les was gazing out the opposite window. Turning, he instantly slammed the control wheel

Margaret Ann dispatching

full forward. It was so close, he said, that he really didn't think we could possibly miss. After their heartbeats had settled down, Les said he told his son, "If anything like that ever happens again, you do what you have to do… then you holler, DAD!"

Thanks 'young Bergsma', for saving all of our lives!

CHAPTER 30

The Woodshed

You might not believe it but I need to tell you about my woodshed. Not many woodsheds merit that much talking, right? Pop moved that little building out to our airport in 1959. It served us faithfully until we sold the airport to the Port of Friday Harbor in the early 80s. In 1984 it was destroyed during a massive Federal airport rebuilding project.

During those 24 or more years that the little building sat out by our gas pumps, it served many purposes, not the least of which was as a conspicuous, yet by its 'very conspicuousness' a secure place to hang fresh meat.

The thing was... not having the finances to build a lovely eight-foot high perimeter fence like the Feds would later do, we were forced (for our protection from the marauding deer) to fight back with whatever means were available to us. This situation frequently caused the little woodshed/oil storage building (without windows) to occasionally be overcrowded with hanging venison...but... being the red-blooded Island boys that we were, we just hitched up our jeans and made do. Yep, that's what we did.

During the winter of '59-60' old Charley Carlyle, with the help of Pop and me and our new pilot, Bill Booze, built our long awaited office-passenger terminal. In later years as our passenger traffic increased, an addition was added to the Terminal but originally it was just a building 30 by 30 feet.

For the airport building layout, we used a V design. The Terminal, with its radio dispatch and air traffic advisory, was at the point of the V, the maintenance shop and hangars were all in the background. Anticipating future needs, we wired our new Terminal for 220 electric heat (not that I had any intention of using it). The thing was, our crosswind runway was still surrounded by forest. During strong winds these trees caused some unnecessarily twisty air currents. I wanted those trees out of there. At the time, however, we neither had the money nor the time to start yet another land clearing project.

Human nature being what it is, I figured unless there was a pressing need, we probably would eventually get accustomed to those trees; then they would be there forever... So we built a masonry chimney into the Terminal and installed a wood heater in the lobby. Now... whether we felt like it or not, X number of trees per year were coming down to feed that hungry stove.

Friday Harbor Airport, circa 1962

Although heating with wood was an unrelenting task, it saved us money and soon proved to be a fortunate choice. The thing was, at this particular time, our Island was being served electrically by some very unreliable underwater power cables. Naturally if those cables were going to fail, and they did, it was when they were needed the most— when the frigid Noreaster was howling and everyone had their electric heat going full blast.

Ha! So here was the local airport Terminal all snug and warm, coffee-pot perking on top of the old wood heater, a little putt-putt generator outdoors supplying us with power for our radios and to ring the bells on our telephones! Under such storm conditions practically all Island businesses closed their doors and waited for the juice to come on. Not us, no siree, not us, we were as snug as a bug in a rug!

Of course like everything else, there was a price to be paid for all this comfort. When the worst of the weather was happening, the Terminal's wood heater could not hold overnight against the draft of the howling wind. Consequently, until the weather broke, my alarm was set for 3:30 a.m. In the winter of '68-69, that howling wind lasted for one solid month.

Ah yes, the joys of owning an Island flying company! Fumbling around, dressing in the dark, crawling into a frigid car, driving through the deserted streets of the village out to the black and howling airport; tree limbs, shrubs, loose snow whipping and thrashing. Carry wood in and stoke up the stove. Back into the car and driving down the line of thrashing airplanes, looking for the loose or broken tie down rope. Jumping out, turning one's back against the frigid blast while trying to tighten a frozen rope. Back to the silent house, stoke the wood stove in the living room, strip off and crawl into bed, try snuggling up, the wife gasping, "Stay away! You're like ice!" A few hours of sleep and then back to the airport.

Since these bad winters only came now and then, it usually meant several of our most recently hired pilots would be facing their very first winter of local flying. That put the onus on the rest of us.

During a bad winter, particularly in those days of poor to non-existent airport facilities, flying a light airplane commercially in this Island Archipelago was a tough assignment. Strong, frigid winds would twist and spill down onto cranky little cow pastures and so-called air strips—every landing and takeoff a test of a pilot's skill and nerve. By the successful end of such a day (successful doesn't mean financial, it means without accident), a pilot would know by the weariness in his bones whether or not he had earned his keep.

Talking about the benefits of wood heat… I only once regretted going that route. That happened on one of those wonderfully clear, cold and sunny winter days that we occasionally have.

Margaret Ann had come out to the airport with our two little children, Steve and Susie. As usual, I was on the far side of the property cutting wood. If I had been falling trees, Margaret Ann would have kept the children out of harm's way. Since I was just buzzing up the logs, she and the children walked over to where I was working.

One hundred feet or so away from me was a big Douglas Fir windfall, its huge uprooted disc of roots and dirt forming a perfect windbreak and sun-drenched place for the children to play in. I stopped for a few minutes to watch… and to enjoy the hot coffee Margaret Ann had brought for me. It had been a tough old winter. The children were tickled to be out of the house (Margaret Ann too) and were having a ball playing in the dirt with their little toy airplane and car.

In a few minutes I went back to work, refreshed and happy to have my family with me. Working alone, I suppose a person gets lonesome without realizing it. Now, having them here with me, it just seemed to make everything right with the world.

Sometime later, evidently much later than I realized, I moved over to work on the big windfall. Finishing with the limbing and stacking into burn piles, I started at the tree's top, advancing down the trunk, sawing off block after block of stove-length wood. Apparently this tree had been down for several years for the wood was seasoned and beautiful.

Finally I was down to sawing off blocks within 15 or 20 feet of the tree's root mass. Without warning the whole thing started to move. Slowly at first, the remaining tree trunk and its root mass started to tip upright, then... with a swish it reared up and crashed down into its original hole.

For a moment I was just startled, then the horrible thought, "The kids! My God, the kids!" I dropped my saw and ran to the base of the tree. It weighed tons. Anybody or anything caught under it would be instantly crushed.

I stopped... Margaret Ann's car was gone. For the first time I looked at my watch. It had been more than two hours since she and the children were there.

That evening she told me she had thought I saw them when they left. I didn't. She even honked the car horn when they drove away. With the chainsaw howling, I didn't hear it.

Experiences like that could make a person's hair turn gray. My wife would say, "Yeah, what hair?"

Oh well...

CHAPTER 31

Some Ground Emergencies

Our winters in the San Juan Islands are normally quite mild; wet with lots of wind, but quite mild. Consequently, since wet and mild was our norm, such things as engine pre-heat equipment were not even a part of our vocabulary. Not only did we lack pre-heat equipment for operating in sub-freezing temperatures but like most commuter airline operators, we suffered from a constant turnover of pilots.

I'm not blaming those young and ambitious pilots for using us as a stepping stone to the 'big office in the sky,' but I'll have to admit there were times when we began to feel like nothing more than a pilot training base for the major airlines.

This pilot turnover meant we were invariably caught by that occasional bad winter with some of our new pilots inexperienced in winter flying. So... when that occasional bad winter did strike, we who were without pre-heat and who had several new pilots on the payroll... yes, we had to really scramble to provide an on time, safe and reliable air service.

Just getting cold engines started without burning the place down—that in itself was a real challenge. So here we are... it was one of those crystal clear, freezing cold days with a cracking 20 to 30 knot wind blowing out of the northeast. The chill factor was well below zero. One of our new pilots, a young man from a warmer climate, was about to depart on one of our local workman flights. This was his first taste of winter flying in the Islands.

An hour before, this same pilot had flown another short flight. On completion of that flight, he had parked his airplane upwind of the Terminal, its nose pointed into the wind. He had now been assigned to another flight using the same aircraft. In the time-lapse between flights the frigid wind had thoroughly chilled his aircraft engine.

I'm in my office working on the Company's proposed spring and summer flight schedules and unaware of what's going on outside. There was a knock on my door and Dan Weber, the dispatcher, leaned in and said, "I think we have a problem."

"What's happening," I asked as we hurried out into the lobby. "Our new pilot was going to pick up some Power Company men on Lopez but he can't get the engine started," Dan answered.

I take one look, seize a fire extinguisher and without a coat, rush for the airplane. The pilot is cranking and cranking; gas is running out of the engine cowl; the carburetor is flooded. If that engine backfires, the plane will catch fire. Being directly upwind from our Terminal, it could mean both the loss of the airplane and the Terminal!

Just as I reach the airplane, BANG! The engine and cowling are enveloped in flames. The pilot jumps out. Shoving the extinguisher nozzle up inside the engine cowl I blast away. It is nip and tuck… just as the extinguisher starts running out of juice the fire goes out… but only momentarily.

Pop! It is burning again! Now the fire has entered the defroster tubes and flames are shooting up on the inside of the windshield. As I frantically exhaust what's left in my extinguisher, I have a terrible sinking feeling in the pit of my stomach—we are about to lose.

Amazingly, the fire goes out; but again, only

momentarily. Pop! It is burning again! Margaret Ann runs out and hands me another extinguisher. The fire is out... the fire is burning again. What the blankety blank hell is going on? I look into the cabin at the controls. Until he was interrupted, the pilot in trying to start a cold engine, had been doing the right thing; he had been using the manual primer-pump to squirt gas into the intake manifold. The pilot is gone but the pump is still off its seat and continuing to siphon a steady stream of fuel to the fire. Every time I knock the flames down, pop! The hot metal ignites the gas again. I close the pump and the fire is out.

We tow the plane to the shop. A new windshield and a new ignition harness, a careful inspection and the plane is ready to fly again. We were damn lucky!

Again—same pilot, same freeze up. It is early morning and the wind and freezing cold are continuing. The new pilot has been assigned to a Seattle charter. Good, that will take him out of the strong wind area of the Islands for several hours.

I'm assigned to the mail run. As I cautiously taxi my empty and vulnerable Cessna 206 downwind and downhill (a bad combination), past our buildings and towards the south end of the runway for takeoff, I see our pilot and his Seattle passenger walk out to the gas pit and get into their airplane.

Eventually, airplanes will be able to taxi on all sides of the fueling pit. Right now, however, with the pit area under construction, that is not possible. It requires that airplanes, after fueling, be manually pushed back from the construction area before engines are started.

I can't believe what I am seeing! Instead of pushing back, our pilot and his passenger have climbed into the plane and are now starting the engine. Good Lord, that means he is about to attempt a sharp, high-powered, downhill, downwind, twisting turn. With the narrow tricycle landing gear of the high winged Cessna, the steep slope of the ground and this wind, it is definitely a turnover, wrecked airplane situation!

I cannot stop and warn him. With my stripped out, empty airplane and the gusting, fierce wind on my tail, I am walking a fine line myself. Frantically I try to call the pilot on my radio—no answer. What a helpless feeling! Suddenly, there he is on the radio, calling me! He says there is something wrong with his trim tab; he can't move it.

Thank God! I tell him to stay right there. I know what the trouble is. I will come back and fix it. "It will only take a minute, okay?"

"Okay," he answers.

Whew! Thank heavens for a bit of frozen moisture in the trim tab's screw jack… it just saved an airplane!

Unable to stop, I continue to slowly creep downhill on the steep taxiway, my plane shuddering in the wind gusts. I debate on how to safely turn this airplane of mine around. I decide to wait until reaching the intersection of the taxiway and the runway. There I will have more room to make a wide, slow, cautious turn. But I must hurry; that pilot might get restless.

I reach the runway and slowly swing into the wind… oops, OOPS! the swinging wing begins to fly; crunch! The lower wing and nose (and the propeller) meet the asphalt. The plane is standing on its wing and nose; the next gust could turn it over.

I rip off my safety belt, hoping to get out and put my weight on the high-wing strut. Just as I get a leg out of the door a heavy gust picks the plane up, flips it over and sails it and me across the runway like a Frisbee, smashing it upside down onto the frozen ground.

Talk about helpless! I see it coming but I am unbelted

and airborne. The ground greets the outside of the windshield at precisely the same instant as my right shoulder contacts the inside. Damn, boys, that frozen ground is hard! And a quarter inch of broken Plexiglas doesn't provide much cushion.

My back is so painful it is hard to breathe with anything more than shallow gasps. I roll out of the door and onto the bottom of the wing. I hear the town fire siren begin to wail. The upside down fuselage of the airplane protects me from the direct blast of the wind. Hank Brown, our chief pilot, drives up in a car and helps me in. We drive to the Terminal. My wife is there. It hurts too damned much. I don't want to hug or shake hands with anybody.

Big, good-natured ex football player Gale Carter bursts in. "Roy," he shouts, "So glad to see you are all right," and he grabs me and gives me a big hug. He really felt bad when he heard my gasp. Thanks anyway Gale, I know you really meant it.

Fire trucks arrive. Everybody is crowding into our little Terminal. Everybody wants to shake hands or hug me. I get my throbbing back against the wall. Dr. Heath roars up in his little English Austin. He was at home on the far side of the Island when informed of an airplane crash at the airfield. Having no details and fearing the worst, he has come at high speed, nearly becoming a casualty himself when his speeding little car and the howling wind met in the open sweep of the valley.

Doc gingerly feels my back, diagnosing it as torn muscles. As a precaution, however, he suggests I ride into the office with him for an x-ray. Weakly waving goodbye to the rapidly swelling crowd of concerned citizens, Doc and I head for town. As we round the church corner I glance up and see the grade school flag at half-mast. I say to Doc, "Looks like I fooled them. It didn't kill me." Doc chuckles

228

and says, "Really Roy! Former President Harry Truman died this morning."

Guess that put me in my place! Me and old Harry.

Our new pilot weathered the winter and became one of our fine Island flyers.

CHAPTER 32

The Stuart Island Tragedy

Talking about past winters in the San Juans, I have to tell you about the Hendron family and the Stuart Island tragedy. It happened during the winter of 1961-62.

The Hendrons, with their six children, had moved to Stuart Island to caretake the Paull Farm where we used to land. They had been chosen for that job because they had three children of grade-school age at the time. The Lighthouse Keeper's wife was a teacher and was home schooling her own two children. Since the State required a minimum of five children to warrant the hiring of a teacher and opening of a school, the three additional children allowed the school to reopen after being closed for some time. It's amazing the difference that school activities can make to a community, especially an isolated one like Stuart.

The Hendrons had a boat with them at Stuart as well as a car parked at Roche Harbor. It was Christmas vacation time, and they were planning to have Christmas together on Stuart. Their oldest daughter was in her first year of High School in Bellevue, Washington where she was boarding with friends. She took a Greyhound bus up to Bellingham, where I picked her up and flew her out to Stuart on our afternoon schedule.

This was the first time this large family had been apart. The arrival of the little kids' greatly missed 'second mommy' was met with much crying and tears both by the kids and the adults. As I prepared to depart, Mrs. Hendron called out, "Roy did you know that you and I are cousins?" Through our Aunt Mildred I had been informed of that just the day before. It was quite a thrill for me. My wife and I had moved out here for this flying job not knowing or of being related to anyone. In those days if you weren't related to half the Island population you were an outsider.

I went over and gave Frances a hug, shook hands with her husband Jim and each of their kids. The Hendrons insisted that Margaret Ann and I and our family come and visit them during the Holidays... I promised we would. When I got home and told Margaret Ann about the invite she was about as excited as I was.

It was not to be... Flying wise, the weather turned bad... fog, right down to the mast. The Hendrons had planned to bring their daughter over in their boat after Christmas and send her to Seattle with us... she didn't come. The only communications with Stuart Island were in emergency situations... through the telephone with the Coast Guard in Port Angeles and then the Coast Guard would radio to the Stuart Island Lighthouse.

As far as we knew we simply had a pesky weather situation but not an emergency. I figured the Hendrons had probably come across in their boat and taken their daughter to Bellevue with their car on the ferry.

January 3rd... the Stuart Island schoolteacher was on the radio and phone-connection from the Lighthouse to me. "Did I know where the Hendrons were, the kids have missed two days of school." I said, "No, we have been unable to fly... they probably took their daughter back to Bellevue." The schoolteacher said, "No, I have called down there... their friends and relatives in Bellevue have not seen them... the girl did not show up for school."

Law enforcement was notified and the search began. The Canadians were also notified. Our Sheriff determined that the Hendron family had been in Friday Harbor on the day before Christmas ... the older boy and his Dad both had gotten haircuts. They had all done some shopping. The Hendron automobile was found at its usual spot, parked at Roche Harbor... the boat was gone --- evidently it had never gotten to Stuart Island. The school teacher and her husband went to the Hendron home on Stuart... dirty dishes and dried food were still on the table... unopened presents were under the Christmas tree.

A week later the Canadians called... on a beach on Vancouver Island was the burned out hulk of a double-ended dory, similar in description to the Hendron boat. Our sheriff and others went there. It was the Hendron boat and in the bottom of the boat was the burned body of a boy child. No trace of the rest of the family was ever found.

Most people who analyzed the circumstances believed that the boat had exploded during refueling on the way back to Stuart. One resident of Roche Harbor, Mrs. Ruben Tarte, reported seeing a red flare-up on the far side of Pearl Island on the night in question. Tony Paull, whose home the Hendrons were caretaking, had gone back and forth to Roche Harbor on Hendron's boat several times. He felt that Hendron had little respect for the explosive properties of gasoline. The Hendron boat was powered by one of those slow turning, long shaft, six blade English outboard motors. It had a small capacity gas tank on the top of the motor... which didn't have the range to make the round trip to Roche and back without refueling. Hendron carried a five-gallon can of fuel along and didn't bother topping off the tank when the boat was tied at the Roche dock but would wait until they ran out of gas in mid channel on the way back... and then as the boat rolled and pitched, slopped fuel in the tank... spilling gas over the hot cylinder and down into the boat. Tony was a long-time airplane pilot and commercial boat

skipper. The careless way Hendron handled gasoline scared
Tony, and he tried to warn him about playing with fire....
But Hendron said something to the effect that there was no
danger as long as there was adequate air circulation.

My God, they all paid a terrible price. The only light
was from their burning boat—they were surrounded by
blackness... miles to nowhere... in those days no homes
on the channel shores... no other boats... the kids usually
wore life jackets but not the adults... burned and freezing...
I had nightmares about it for weeks.

CHAPTER 33

The Waldron Arrangement

For many years, it was a special challenge to provide air service to some of the small outlying islands that were without telephone or radio communications. Take Waldron Island for example---

An active sea captain, Jim Lovering, lived with his wife and daughter on Waldron Island. Jim was dependent on the Air Service to relay any urgent calls to him from his shipping company.

I never asked Captain Lovering, but I would think that his company would have kept him pretty much informed via the three-times-a week U.S. mail to Waldron. However, the standing agreement between the Air Service and all the Waldron residents and their guests, was that we would accept important telephone calls on their behalf and forward them via a weighted streamer and note direct to their house on Waldron, if necessary.

For example, if a Waldron woman was in one of the Bellingham hospitals having a baby, the hospital would phone the Air Service with this kind of information "Baby boy born 8 a.m. today, 7 lbs., mother and baby doing fine—mother and baby wish to book on your Wednesday a.m. flight to Waldron Island."

These aerial announcements were fun. I'd carefully check the wind direction and drift, as well as the direction of the sun. Then I'd howl down and shake up their shingles, haul up and throw out (upwind) a partly unrolled roll of toilet paper (blue for a boy, pink for a girl). The people would be down there, running around, jumping up and down. I remember Bob Burn in particular, chasing the drifting, twirling, colorful toilet paper (and winding it up for future use). Then I would drop the message (strip of white cloth, with small rock and message knotted in the end), just heavy enough to prevent much wind drift but light enough to not hurt anyone. Then everyone would be at the Waldron Airstrip waiting for the mother and baby at the scheduled time.

Ray, a retired mail carrier and Mary Tiberghien lived on Waldron Island. They were from the Massachusetts area. Ray's elderly sister from Boston was visiting Ray and Mary on Waldron. The sister had never been to such a primitive area before (no electricity, no phone, etc.) The sister was expecting an important call. Ray had assured her not to worry—the local Air Service (me) would receive the call and drop a note to her—which I did. They got the note. The sister departed.

Next summer, Ray and Mary went to Boston on vacation. Big chuckles. . . on the sister's very formal Boston mantle was a rock, a note, and a strip of my old T-shirt. The sister was very proud—she was telling people "that's how they communicate on the Northwest frontier."

This is how we served the small islands from the 1950s into the 1970s. Communications improved even more from 1966 to 1979, when we had the mail contact serving the small islands. That is a story in itself.

Tom Wilson was a new operator in Anacortes with a charter operation who wanted the mail contract. I flew over to meet him and tell him I had been here for 15 years longer than him and also wanted the contract for the Islands. His response—"If you get it, no way will you land at my field in Anacortes." My response—"If you get the contract, no way will you land on my private airport at Friday Harbor." This obviously wasn't going to work. After a couple of drinks, we agreed to form a new company called Island Mail, Inc, with each owning 50% and we would bid it together. We did get the contract. Tom would do the eastern islands, including Orcas, Blakely, Decatur and Sinclair, and I would take the western Islands—San Juan, Lopez, Shaw, Waldron and Stewart.

We would fire the Bushman up in the morning darkness of winter six days a week, fly to Anacortes to load up the mail for the western islands, then return via Lopez to Friday Harbor. We would then use the smaller airplanes to deliver the mail to the outlying islands, as our Air Service continued to be the glue binding our Island communities together.

Home delivery on Waldron Island's West beach.
Mary Tiberghien (left) welcomes her husband Ray home.

CHAPTER 34

Pilotage and the First 172

The owners of Bellingham Flying Service, Earl Erickson, Cecil Pitts and Paul Mitchell, besides running an aircraft maintenance business, were also involved in crop spraying. Earl ran the maintenance part, Paul and Cecil the flying end of things

Eventually Cecil went his own way and the two remaining partners replaced their five biplane sprayers with two helicopters. Amazingly, the two helicopters, now flown by Paul and his son, could do as much in the same period of time as the five aircraft had been able to do.

For example, Paul said he could land in the field alongside his tanker truck, refuel, reload the spray, and be back working in about the time it took an airplane to fly back to the airport for his next load. Also by not having to zoom up over utility wires, make a big turn-around on the end of each pass, etc., the helicopter could spray field corners, borders and areas practically under the utility lines in less time and with far less risk.

Bellingham Flying Service also had a Cessna dealership. It was in 1957 or 1958 when the boys took delivery of their first Cessna 172 demonstrator. This Cessna four-place 172 was in direct competition with the out-of-production Stinson Voyagers that we were operating. Lots of little digs started coming our way (all in fun?) "Why don't you treat your passengers to a flight in a modern airplane?" etc.

With varying degrees of trepidation I eventually submitted to this sales pitch; traded in one of our faithful Stinson Voyagers, N-9047K, for our first Cessna 172.

The very first night of the very first day that we owned this 172, Dr. Heath called about a patient with an apparent heart attack on Lopez Island. At the moment the only equipment I had available was the new Cessna and our two-place Cessna 140 trainer (I don't remember where the other Voyager or the Bushman was... probably on the mainland for engine overhaul).

Anyway, I got the new Cessna out and the doctor and I hurriedly taxied out for takeoff. Of no particular concern was an area of mud lying between the hangar and the runway. Since I had been taxiing the tailwheeled Stinsons through that mud area all day, I never gave the matter a second thought.

Boy, the price one pays for experience!

The little nose wheel dropped down into the mud and 'BANG, BANG! one ruined propeller! And one grounded airplane!

Good Lord! No ambulance plane, now not even a four seater

... all that was left was the two-seat trainer!

With the little trainer's one landing light, the doctor and I found the Lopez landing strip in the dark and we landed okay.

I accompanied the doctor and driver of the waiting car to the troubled home. The person in distress was a craggy featured, fine old seafaring man. His wife had died and he was living by himself. The house was small and as neat as a pin. Several beautifully handcrafted models of sailing ships sat on the mantel.

After a careful examination, Dr. Heath said the old fellow should go to a mainland hospital that very night. In view of the aircraft situation, it was going to take several trips.

We all rode back to the airport together, the driver and the old Captain waiting in the car while I flew the doctor back to Friday Harbor. Finding our unlighted Friday Harbor runway with my one-eyed trainer wasn't nearly as bad as finding Lopez, the Friday Harbor airport being right next to the lighted town.

I dropped off the doctor, flew back and found Lopez again; picked up the old fellow (fortunately he could walk) and then flew him to Bellingham and to the waiting ambulance.

By the time I flew back, found and landed on our unlighted home strip and got the plane put away, it was 1:00 o'clock in the morning. I was angry with myself for ever considering a tricycle landing geared airplane when our strips were still so crude... and I was angry with Paul Mitchell for talking me into it. I was so angry and frustrated that I telephoned Mitchell up; got him out of bed and gave him a withering blast concerning that no good, useless, thin-skinned, lousy, tomato can of an airplane that he had sold to me. Also that I would be at his Airport by dawn to take back my Stinson Voyager; and further, that I wanted him to come out to Friday Harbor with a propeller and get his Wichita abortion off my airport.

Paul was a fine person and I knew even through my anger that he was a true friend. Without raising his voice he calmly said, "Each airplane design has its good points and maybe some that are not so good, depending on what your needs are. But the airplane should not be blamed for "Poor Pilotage!"

EEEEEEOW!

The wife shot up out of bed and exclaimed, "What happened?"

Anyway… things were under control by daylight and I had to agree with Mitchell; you can't blame the airplane or someone else for your own mistakes. Of course Mitchell didn't know about this 5:00 o'clock in the morning revelation of mine.

When I walked into the Bellingham Air Service waiting room that morning, Paul and his two business partners, Earl and Cecil, were over in the corner grouped around the old oil stove—no smiles, no morning greeting. Paul's eyes were furtive, his face haggard and he had a runny nose. Looked to me like he might have missed some sleep.

I apologized to Paul for the 1:00 a.m. tirade, ordered a new propeller, turned on my heel and walked out. In a few days our jovial relationship had returned to normal.

Our passengers loved the new plane and as long as I exercised "Good Pilotage," (by keeping out of mud holes) Paul's tomato can proved to be a low maintenance, money maker (under-powered and with slow reaction controls… but still a good airplane).

A number of years later Paul was flying one of his helicopters in the Cascade Mountains and was killed when his engine quit and he auto-rotated into the tops of the towering timber. Paul's two partners, Cecil Pitts and Earl Erickson, also died rather early but from natural causes, however.

CHAPTER 35

The Post Office Dedication

Another big event during 1961 and 1962 was the controversy before the building and dedication of a new Post Office in Friday Harbor. It involved our Air Service in some interesting ways. Let me tell you about it.

As was common in those days, the Post Office would often lease space in small communities from a private business or homeowner before there was the population to warrant a new building. In 1951, the U.S. Postal Service concluded such an agreement with Elmer and Sarah Marble, owner of Marble's Hardware and Grocery Store on Spring Street (now the Island Studios). A ten-year contract was signed for use by the Post Office of 1,600 square feet in that store.

That arrangement worked fine for some years, but by the late 1950s the town was continuing to grow and the Post Office needed more space. Plans were made for a new Post Office near the Court House, on the corner of First and Court Streets. But since construction was delayed, the Post Office requested extension of its lease beyond its termination. A short extension was agreed upon, but by the winter of that year, the location of the new Post Office was still a naked lot and Elmer Marble was worried about not having that 1,600 feet available to him for his own remodeling before the next summer season. Requests for further lease extensions for the Post Office were refused. A local firestorm was ignited on the morning of January

1, 1962, when Elmer padlocked the front door and refused entry to the Post Office. The news spread quickly all the way to the East Coast and the federal government, which soon seized the 1,600 square feet for continued operation of the Friday Harbor Post Office for a six-month period until the end of June. The padlock was removed on January 2, but the standoff soon became a legal matter as Marble brought suit in federal court in Bellingham for damages.

Meanwhile, construction for the new Post Office got underway, and plans were made for a big dedication ceremony on June 2 of that year. Dignitaries would be coming to Friday Harbor, and the Post Office planned a special cachet for collectors with pictures of a fishing boat, ferry and airplane as well as the new building and a map showing Bellingham, Victoria and Seattle in relation to Friday Harbor. All mail processed on June 2 was to be sent out by air to speed this special cachet to collectors.

Our Air Service looked forward to a big opportunity to show off our new airport, and especially a 12-place Lockheed Electra which we had just purchased a month earlier. We planned to send our own town dignitaries down to Seattle on June 2 in the Electra to welcome out-of-town guests, and to have a party at the Friday Harbor Airport after the dedication of the Post Office.

The morning of the 2nd was a wild scene. A strong storm was blowing in from the southeast. That was not our only problem. A phone call from Seattle soon informed us that our four passengers there were refusing to fly with us and that the dedication was being cancelled. The reason given was that they would not fly with us since we were refusing to allow a new competitor from Orcas Island to bring them into Friday Harbor. That's another story of itself.

A few months earlier, a pilot and his wife had arrived

on Orcas and set up a competing air service, charging $9.00 one-way to Seattle (our fares were $10.00) and leaving 10 minutes before each of our scheduled flights. The pilot had a Grumman Widgeon and a Beechcraft Bonanza for these flights. He had leased the Widgeon from its owners in Denver. We told him to take his operation elsewhere. In order to further undermine our well-established Air Service, he waited until the 2nd to tell the Seattle contingent that he had been refused landing rights at Friday Harbor Airport. I was thunderstruck hearing this news and their anger on the phone. The owner of the local newspaper, *The Journal*, Robert Hartzog, suggested that we call Senator Scoop Jackson in Washington, D.C. for help. I wasn't used to making such calls, but Hartzog agreed to do so. His access to the Senator made a big difference right away. Brushing past the Senate's switchboard operator there, he was soon on the phone with the Senator himself, whose first question was "Who in hell has put another padlock on the door in Friday Harbor?!" The circumstances were explained, and the Senator agreed to fix the problem on the spot. He called the Seattle group, told them that the Electra was on its way, and the dedication would proceed on schedule.

Since Bob Nichols had a lot of multi-engine time, he was flying the left seat as we took off in the Electra into the storm. Ceilings were low and the air wild. We made most of the flight to Seattle at or below 500 feet. We wondered what we'd find at the other end since we'd been told just before that the Seattle group wouldn't fly with us for any reason. Our *Journal* friend had assured us, however, that "Scoop has fixed all that."

In Seattle we met our four passengers who were obviously very angry. Fortunately, our four-member greeting party (including our Mayor) was able to establish some communication on the way back. Our fast-moving storm was still a problem. We climbed to 11,000 feet in an attempt to get above it, but were unsuccessful. We poked out into the clear over Port Townsend and Hooray!. . . the sun was shining on the San Juans. The wind had shifted to the southwest, and our next problem was a roaring crosswind at Friday Harbor.

What to do? The crosswind was much too much for the Electra and our small main runway. Our grass crosswind strip was only 30 feet wide with barbwire fences on both ends and only about 1,000 feet of slippery grass runway. We did not want to wreck our new airplane, especially with all eyes on us. Diverting to Bellingham would only delay the dedication, and require us to use the smaller airplanes to bring back our ten people three at a time in this screaming crosswind, now gusting over 40. Should we go back to Seattle, or cancel everything?

We circled over Friday Harbor taking some time to decide. The sun was out and our passengers were enjoying the view, including the ocean all white with whitecaps. Pilot Bob wanted to try the crosswind strip, but it was short and we were really loaded. By now there was quite a contingent at the airport watching our arrival, including a photographer next to the runway from *Pacific Northwest Aviation* who would capture the whole landing on film. So here we were, coming right at him in wild turbulence off the trees. How we missed the fence, I'll never know. It seemed we had a wheel on each side of a fence post as we went over it. Bob set her down perfectly. . . slamming on the brakes, we slid and slid, and finally stopped 200 feet short of the runway's end. Soon we had a happy group all around the airplane congratulating Bob on a tremendous landing.

Everyone then went to the Post Office, where the School Band was playing and a crowd had gathered for the dedication. Postmaster Walter Ahrend came up to me and

Open House at Friday Harbor Airport with new Lockheed Electra

said " Roy, since you've hauled all these people up here for our ceremony, we're going to come out and really give you a blast at the Airport." So when the dedication was over, all these people came out, had coffee and cake. The sun was out and everyone had a great time. Bob flew our visitors back to Seattle in the sunshine and we had all kinds of good publicity for the Air Service, including a two-page spread in the next paper.

So that's the famous Post Office story. By the way the new "Air Service" on Orcas soon departed. It turned out that he had had brief failed attempts in Alaska where he had come in and undercut other operators. He had even run up $17,000 in unpaid charges on the Widgeon and his other operations during his short stay on Orcas. He left with his wife without any notice several days later, leaving a beautiful Widgeon and all his bills behind on Orcas. The Denver owners of the Widgeon had to pay $17,000 to get their airplane back when it was put up for auction soon thereafter by the Sheriff to pay these bills. This phantom "operator" had leased the Widgeon for only one month then disappeared over the horizon. His departure from Orcas was evidently just one more of his disappearing acts.

CHAPTER 36

Even Busier With More Airplanes

In the late '50s our flying equipment consisted of three Stinsons (the six-place Bushman N27782 and two four-place Voyagers.) We traded in one Voyager in '59 for our first of two tricycle geared Cessna 172's, a 1957 and the next year a 1958 model.

As with all flying machines, everything is a trade-off, some superior features, some not. The Cessnas were all metal, superior to the Stinson's relatively short-life fabric. The Cessnas had better visibility for both the pilot and the passengers and they were roomier. Unlike the Stinson Voyagers, the Cessna baggage area was part of the cabin. With a Cessna stripped out for freight, this inclusive baggage-area feature gave us a longer length of cabin for payload.

Compared to the Stinson, the Cessna was a much easier airplane for passengers to climb in and out of. Considering our short, rapid shuttle hops that was an important factor. This increased ease of access was not only due to the cabin floor being level with the ground (tricycle gear versus tailwheel) but also the doors were much wider and the cabin floor was flush with the door sill.

With the Stinson's narrow door and high sill, it was necessary for a person, when mounting, to rear back and kick a leg in... as though you were jumping a hurdle. With the advent of hot pants, we pilots sure missed those Stinsons. Yes siree, we surely did. And we missed those

Stinsons when it was necessary to land in, and get back out of small muddy fields or when the wind was swirling and twisting.

But anyway… the Stinsons were being phased out in favor of the more modern Cessnas.

All but one, the Bushman. Our old Stinson Bushman stayed with us to the end. In all the years we were in business, we always found jobs for that airplane. It was for many years the only airplane in the County big enough to carry a stretcher case (with attendants). During that era it served as the 'Boeing 747' of all our passenger and freight flights.

Medical evacuation flight in the Bushman

Even when the six and seven passenger Cessna 206's and 207's were introduced with their better forward visibility and thus the more desirable night and bad weather evacuation aircraft… even then the Bushman kept right on earning her keep, hauling the daily workmen and their gear, the U.S. mail and dropping supplies in the mountains.

In 1961 we traded our last Stinson Voyager in on what proved to be a hard luck 1961 model Cessna 172 (33 X-

Roy with Dr. Heath and patient in the Bushman

ray). This 1961 model was supposed to correct most of the earlier 172 models' deficiencies. For example… the early models would fall on their tails if you put the back seat passengers and luggage in first. Also the early models, because of tall landing gear legs, were pretty ' tippy' when taxiing crosswind. Another thing, the instrument panels in the early models were too small for all the new electronic gear that was now required.

Consequently the new 1961 model's landing gear was shortened and placed farther aft and the instrument panel was now huge. That solved the panel-crowding problem, but we lost some of our great over-the-nose visibility.

The most noticeable outside change to this 1961 model, besides the lower landing gear, was the change from the traditional straight up and down vertical stabilizer and rudder to a 'swept-back' configuration. Sweeping the tail back did two things for us, one good, the other bad. It made the plane longer and thus more directionally stable; but... by making the airplane longer the poor thing wouldn't fit into our economy hangars! At least without the spinner and propeller sticking outside.

The Bushman over Bellingham Bay

Poor 33 X-ray; had to sleep with its nose hanging out of the hangar and always seemed to be in the wrong place at the wrong time. For example: one stormy morning Bob Nichols and our newest pilot, Dick Palmer, were flying 33 X-ray and another 172 on the Bellingham schedule. I was dispatching. Being momentarily short on airplanes and since the return Bellingham schedule would only require one airplane, I instructed Palmer, on landing at Bellingham, to unload and return immediately to Friday Harbor.

From what the boys told me later, this is what happened. By the time the two planes were on final approach to the Bellingham runway the wind had increased in velocity. Although the landings and the taxiing were a bit tricky, the boys pulled it off okay. As soon as they were unloaded

Bob put his full attention into taking care of the passengers. Dick cranked up his engine, per orders, and started taxiing out for his flight back to Friday Harbor.

In about 60 seconds new pilot Dick would know, as he crawled out of the wreckage of his airplane (33 X-ray), that in the future this was one of those times when a pilot tells the boss, "If you need me, ring the coffee shop because that's where I'll be until this wind goes down."

Poor 33 X-ray; the ribs on the top of her wings were crushed, her propeller was a twisted pretzel, her tail was mashed and her fuselage was buckled. Seeing as how things in the shop were pretty quiet, we decided to rebuild 33 X-ray. A number of months and many, many dollars later, there she was out on the ramp, new paint job and all!

Traffic for the Electra never materialized. In the meantime, the demand for our small airplanes was increasing and we were short of aircraft. So we decided to sell the Electra and purchase two 1964 model Cessna 172s. Quite a design change; the 1964s had the chopped down back with the aft cabin window.

So now it is springtime; the sun is shinning, the wind is calm, our Friday Harbor Airport is a buzz of activity. Margaret Ann is dispatching pilot Terry Holt with a load of passengers in one of our new 172s and he is just cranking up his engine. Suddenly a little, apparently insignificant whirlwind starts spinning there on the ramp area… it picks up an empty airplane alongside of Terry and smashes the plane upside down almost on top of him.

One guess… yep, 33 X-ray! Reduced to a pile of wreckage!

The last time I saw that poor thing she was on a truck headed for the ferry and a Seattle bone-yard. We got $2,000 for the wreckage. Good bye 33 XRAY!

Daily activities at Friday Harbor Airport

In a way we were relieved to see the last of 33 X-ray. The pilots called it the 'lead sled.' Even before it had ever suffered damage, it never felt light and responsive on the controls. Just one of those things, I guess.

During the '60s we bought two Cessna 182's and two Cessna six-place 206's. We also replaced the three early 172's (the '57 and '58 models and the busted up '61 model) with two 1964 models.

Although we were getting busier all the time in the early '60s, there were still so many things we needed. Not just desired, but needed. Runway lights for example, we really needed them but it would require over a mile of ditching and direct burial power cable, plus 22 weatherproof light fixtures.

Another major problem—our airport's graveled runway, taxiway and graveled loading area were giving us troubles.

The thing was, we were moving into newer aircraft (Cessna 172's) which were equipped with nose gears instead of the conventional tailwheels. These new planes were most 'passenger-desirable' but their low clearance propellers were sucking up grit and gravel, which was causing major propeller blade damage.

Since all our future airplanes would have this same tricycle landing gear configuration, there remained only one logical solution—hardtop the whole bloody airport! I shuddered to think of the cost.

For several summer seasons we forestalled the inevitable by hiring the County Road Department to come in with thousands of gallons of hot oil and their spreader truck (and their roller). This did a pretty good job of pinning down the loose stuff, but the program was expensive and had to be repeated every year.

Since the County was interested in air transportation and in the new airport we were constructing, and since there was no one in the County in the asphalt business, the County felt justified in making us a proposal. They offered the oil, the crushed rock, the men and the machinery to put two layers of 'hot mix' on our runway, taxiway, access road, car parking area and aircraft loading area. They would do this for cost. I can't remember what that totaled but it was less than $20,000. Considering the size of the job, their offer was very reasonable.

True... but good Lord, it was a staggering amount of additional debt to take on! What could we do? Sooner or later we'd have to do it. Damage wise... better sooner than later.

Cecil Carter and Bob Gregory at the San Juan County Bank were getting mighty tired of me showing up with that 'Give-Me' look on my face. Reluctantly they granted the additional loan.

For us, the decade of the '60s was a time of action and expansion. It wasn't just us; the whole area was beginning to boom. It was as though it had taken everybody the decade of the '50s to recover from the trauma and turmoil of the terrible '40s.

Roy with Bob Nichols (left) and Bill Booze (right)

Now with the '60s it was "UP, UP, AND AWAY!" Company wise we had a number of good things going for us. For one thing we had great publicity. Bob Nichol's wife, Lorrie, was writing an interesting weekly column for *The Journal* based on our Air Service activities and our daily clientele. Lorrie's column was called '*Prop Wash*' and it was well written and very popular. More than once one of my passengers, a total stranger, would look at me and say, "Now which one are you?" The first time it happened I was really surprised. One woman hastily added, "We live in New York but we get *The Journal*, so we know all about you boys."

Along with this publicity came a County-wide Awards Night with Island Sky Ferries Inc. receiving a plaque and being declared the County's first recipient of the 'Company of the Year' award. This was held at Rosario Resort on Orcas Island. During the ceremony, Bob Schoen, my former boss, presented me with the wooden airplane propeller that had caused my crash landing on Crane Island in 1949. Shortly thereafter (a year or so) the local Chamber of Commerce awarded a plaque to me as 'Best Boss.'

Roy and Bob Schoen with the wooden propeller

The articles written and the favorable publicity generated by this public recognition were priceless company advertising. Another good thing that happened—Roche Harbor Lime and Cement Company was now a resort. Under the tutelage of the Tarte family, miles of beautiful shoreline were opening up for home sites. Mainland people were buying and building... and flying.

CHAPTER 37

The Seaplane Base

In 1964 we also purchased Bill Savage's seaplane base. Bill was involved in a divorce. He was discouraged. His place was run down. He wanted out. We bought Bill's place of business because I felt having both land and sea would give us an advantage that neither Bill nor I ever had as individual companies. I felt one type of service was bound to compliment the other.

What we received with our purchase was primarily the right to use the location (as long as we kept up the land-lease payments to the Port). Along with the location we got a cedar log seaplane float, a dock leading out to the float and the small office/home Bill had lived in.

Everything was homebuilt, old and needed to be rebuilt, replaced or created.

Ah, the optimism of the uninitiated! We all had visions (especially me I guess) of building up a prosperous, thriving seaplane operation. Bob Nichols, Pappy and I flew into the project with a will.

Following the sale of his place to us, Bill Savage took his seaplane and left for Alaska. Several years later, near Sitka, Alaska, the wing on a seaplane, a Helo-Courier that Bill was flying, came off in rough air and Bill and his two executive passengers spun to their deaths in the timber below. Although there were no witnesses to the accident, there was no question as to the cause; one wing was missing. It was found a quarter mile or more from the rest of the wreckage.

Bill had flown these Islands for 17 years. He and I had some great hunts together. We competed like mad and then when the weather went to pot, we went hunting together. He loved to fly, to play his trumpet for dances, and he was very popular. With Bill's passing, an era passed with him. So long Bill… you will never be forgotten.

In Friday Harbor, Bill had developed quite a technique for overnighting his seaplane (four-place Piper Family Cruiser). To protect his airplane from the dangers of sinking during the night from leaking pontoons… or of being damaged by some errant boat operator, Bill put his airplane 'up' for the night.

The first time I saw him do it, I thought he had flipped his lid. Here he came, straight at the side of his log float; on contact the plane reared its nose up high, then with a burst of power rocked forward and down, the pontoons coming down to rest on the float's plank deck… just as pretty as you please!

To aid in this daily ritual of 'flying to the nest,' Savage had taken an axe and chopped a sloping ramp in the side of his raft, one for each pontoon. To launch his plane, all he had to do was untie it and lift up on the front of the pontoons. Whoop-tee-do, in she slid!

This 'over-nighting' on-top of the float routine Savage used was okay for him, living right there where he could keep an eye on things, but I knew it wasn't going to be satisfactory for us. For one thing, we would not be living there. I wanted to be assured that during our absences, our seaplane was not bobbing around on top of a raft, its delicate tailfeathers hanging out over the water for some boat to back into.

No, if possible, I wanted our airplane to be on terra firma with washing facilities. Unlike Savage's airplane, our airplanes would be all metal and we would want a daily de-salting bath of fresh water.

On shore, next to the seaplane office, were the beginnings of a ramp. We finished it out and planked it over. Only trouble was, the ramp only reached the water during high tide. What we needed was a ramp extension. John Sheasby agreed to build us a four-wheeled carriage. He provided me with its measurements.

During springtime minus tides, with booties and the lower half of my diving suit on, I got down into the shoreline mud and using Sheasby's width dimensions, gathered and piled two rows of rocks for the ramp extension.

Jim Browne backed his cement truck as close as possible and sent down to me a load of special cement. Since my rock/cement job would soon be covered by the incoming tide, Jim had mixed this cement with considerable calcium for a rapid 'set-up.' It worked perfectly. Even today, over 40 years later and in front of a marine park instead of a seaplane base, the remains of my marine railway are still visible.

With new, two inch, mine-type steel rails cradled in the cement and rocks, and spiked up the length of the plank ramp, things were looking up.

Sheasby cut and welded the carriage, 'in-place.' The slope of the ramp was a steep 18 degrees. Sheasby built the carriage to match that slope. In other words, when the carriage was backed down the ramp and into the water, the wheels of the carriage were on the 18-degree slope but the cradle for the airplane was perfectly level with the surface of the water. This enabled the seaplane to float into or out of the cradle without interference.

To power this operation, we had a powerful winch

anchored solidly on shore, at the upper end of the ramp. This winch was powered electrically and controlled from two different locations. One control cable ran down the dock, its control-head on the seaplane float... the other control was carried on the carriage.

Stand-by for a demonstration!

Our seaplane, (first one was a Cessna 172 on 2000 floats) bobbing comfortably alongside the float, had been serviced by our new dockside gas and oil pumper and is now ready for its daily fresh water bath, window job, inspection and securing for the night. That will all come in a few minutes.

Standing alongside the plane, I pick up the pushbutton winch control and looking across the water at the ramp and carriage, I determine all is clear of obstructions. I push the 'down' button. The winch releases its brake, the steep slope and weight of the carriage brings it steadily down the track and into the water.

Sheasby has bolted planks to the bottom and insides of the actual cradle that will hold the airplane... and has installed a one-plank-width walkway around three sides, one foot above the cradle bottom.

I push the stop-button just as the walkways touch the water. That gives me one foot of water in the cradle. Untying the plane, I start the engine and taxi over and into the flooded cradle. Perfect! (John has even installed short plank bumpers on each side of the cradle-entrance, in case the plane is not lined up properly). Stepping out onto the walkway, I secure the airplane's front pontoon cleats to the cradle.

On the front corner of the carriage walkway is a four-foot high steel post. On the top of this post is secured the other winch control, its waterproof power cable lying under water and alongside the track.

Now comes the moment I cherish. Steadied by the steel standard, I stand like George Washington crossing the Delaware, my favorite steed and I bursting out of the water and up the ramp! YAHOO!

At the proper moment, I push the Stop button. The winch's automatic brake locks the carriage in place. I step off and as a safeguard against the unguarded night, secure the carriage to the track with a chain and padlock.

Ah, you will never guess! Turning on the fresh water spicket, the airplane, from one end to the other, is immediately smothered in a shower of fresh water (piping and many nozzles have been installed between the planks of the ramp). We have an automatic airplane wash! Being down on the waterfront and much, much lower than the town's storage tank, we have 100 plus pounds of water pressure! Some deal, hey what!

But let me tell you about the bonus. With the carriage and the airplane up on the 18° ramp, the airplane is sitting way up there on the level. I can walk under the pontoons and inspect every square inch of their bottoms! It's like having a car up on a grease rack. This daily pontoon damage inspection is important when you are operating an airplane in and out, on and off rock-strewn waters and beaches.

The float, the dock, the stairs down to the dock, a car parking area, the office/house, all had to be either created or overhauled. For example, Savage's dock which ran out to the float consisted of just a narrow, aerial walkway… without railings. Besides that, some of the deck plankings were rotten and the pilings holding the whole thing up were on their last legs.

I put the suit and tank on and went for an underwater inspection tour. No, I didn't buy a pig in a poke. I knew, and Bill had told me, that the place would need some major repairs. He was right. The cedar logs under the seaplane float were riddled with Terredos (salt water wood-devouring worms). The heavy chains and concrete anchors that held the float in place were not doing their job. I'll explain.

During this particular era, the ferry dock was in front of the present 'Downrigger' restaurant. This was next door to the Union Oil dock and the seaplane base. Every reverse thrust of the ferryboat's propellers while docking, or forward thrust as they departed, sent a boiling mass of water through the Union Oil dock's pilings and over to bang against Bill's seaplane float. To counter this, Bill had his float secured with two driven pilings plus heavy chains and concrete anchors, or so he thought.

Now it would appear that electrolysis, the old enemy of dissimilar metals in salt water, had destroyed his connecting shackles, and… at some earlier date the action of the water had broken the cable connections from both of his concrete anchors!

Acting on Cleve Vandersluy's advice, we went to the shipyard beach and using 2 x 8's built two, three-foot-square by eight-inch forms for new anchors. As soon as Jim Brown filled them with cement, we inserted in each a stainless steel cable having a braided eye in each end. This doubled the anchor life; if one eye broke off we could use the other.

After a few days of curing, Cleve ran a cable ashore from his work boat, the 'Haida,' and with his winch, snaked our new anchors out to and up alongside his boat. He then transported them down the harbor to the seaplane base. I dove down and hooked up our chains to the anchors.

We hired the Leif Wade/Jack Fairweather piledriving and dock repair service to come in and put several new cedar logs under the float. They also drove new creosote-treated pilings under the dock and replaced some of the beams. The local carpenter, Al Buck, replaced the dock's deck planking for us and built up guardrails the full length of the dock. This business of connecting a stationary dock to a float that moves up and down five to ten feet with each tide change was something a lot of us drylanders hadn't considered. We soon found out how it was done.

The connection between the dock and the float requires a ramp that is structurally strong and built like a section of unsupported bridge. They attach one end of this ramp to the dock with a steel hinge; the other end of the ramp rests on the float below, and is fitted with a roller. As the float rises and falls with the tide, the pitch of the ramp gets steeper or flatter, the lower end of it rolling back and forth on the float's plank deck.

Because of the steep terrain the seaplane base was located on, there was no place for cars to park except on the street above, which was frowned upon. So by building a concrete wall from the office out to and up the property line and by dumping truckloads of dirt and gravel in behind it, we created a level parking lot. This wall, wouldn't you know it, obliterated Savage's steep dirt steps down to the rock. This then required building wooden stairs, with railings, all the way down to the dock.

All the time the above was taking place, the office/apartment project was progressing. This project required, starting with a new tar job on the flat roof, a complete wiring and remodeling throughout. Bob Nichols is a mighty handy man. He did all the rewiring himself.

Fortunately for us the building was basically sound. We tried to keep costs to a minimum but it is hard to do something halfway, right? Anyway, we ended up with a beautiful little office/waiting room with a magnificent marine view. Across the front of the building we built a full-length deck with railing. The rest of the building retained its apartment flavor... with a kitchen, a rest room and a bunkroom.

As our summer employment at the Airfield increased, the seaplane bunkhouse became a home for our single guys. They loved it! They told me about the line of young gals who walked past the door of that seaplane base, especially the 'bored stiff' ones who had spent a required vacation on the boat with Momma and Papa... YeeeeOW! Wonder we got any work out of those boys a-tall!

CHAPTER 38

A Family Emergency on a Stormy Night

Somebody once said that flying for a living was nothing more than hours and hours of boredom occasionally punctuated by moments of shear terror. Ah yes... well you might say it eventually was my turn.

By the time I quit commercial flying in 1979 I had flown night and day for years in all kinds of weather in the Islands. I had also flown 21 summer fire seasons of fire patrol and parachute supply-dropping in the Cascade Mountains of Washington State and five seasons in the Olympic Mountains for the Olympic National Park Service. During those years, sure, there were a few sweaty moments—like when my mechanic put the wrong spark plugs in my airplane engine and I didn't know it until a tight mountain situation required maximum power and all I got was a backfiring engine. Or the time a new dropper opened a chute early and it hung up on our tail and dragged us down.

However, it is one thing for a person who flies for a living to accept the risks that are inherent to his profession, but quite another for innocent people, as passengers, to be unknowingly exposed to violent and extreme dangers.

I got into a situation like that one night in the early '60s during a night medical flight. A mother and her daughter were my passengers and I flew them right into the jaws of death.

During the daylight hours preceding this particular night flight, our northern Puget Sound area was experiencing a rather unusual happening—an influx of violent, unstable air. Consequently, since early afternoon, the other pilots and I had been watching with trepidation a boiling mass of clouds forming over Orcas Island to the north of us and also over the Cascade Mountains to the east.

As we four company pilots, Bill Booze, Bob Nichols, Dick Palmer and I made ready to go home, we stood for a few minutes by our cars warily studying the deteriorating weather. Through the few breaks still remaining in the overcast we could see that many of the clouds had grown to be huge, towering monsters; so high the jet stream was blowing their tops into the classic anvil head shape of the cumulonimbus storm cloud.

"Enough raw energy in one of those monsters to light the city of Seattle," commented chief pilot Booze.

Opening his car door, Nichols took one more look at the building storm and said, "Sure hope nobody has to be flown off the Island tonight."

"Amen to that," Palmer said, "I'm the on-call pilot!"

As the four of us watched, the last rift in the low overcast closed, and the roll of thunder filled the air.

Suddenly looking at his wristwatch, Booze exclaimed, "Oh my God, what time does King's Market close?" Man, you're in trouble," Nichols said, "They close in five minutes!"

With a plaintive, "My wife is going to kill me" and with a screech of rubber, Booze was gone.

Nichols shouted, "Ballgame's on! See you guys tomorrow!"

And we all departed post haste.

When I got home, my wife, Margaret Ann, met me at the door with a worried look on her face. "Janet," she said, "has been hemorrhaging really bad all day. Dr. Heath was here this morning and said he would be back to check on her this evening. I'm really worried; she's so weak."

Margaret Ann and I went upstairs to daughter Janet's bedroom. Janet lay there, barely 13 years old, embarrassed about her female problems, almost as pale as her white bed sheets.

Reaching out a limp hand to me, she said, "Hi, Daddy."

Sometime after supper, Dr. Heath hurried in and was escorted upstairs. He was only up there for a few minutes. Coming down, he said to me, "I know the weather looks threatening, Roy, but this girl needs to be in a hospital where there is a whole blood supply."

As I cleaned the airplane's plexiglass windshield, static electricity popped and snapped, making the hair on my arms prickle. Every nerve in my body seemed to be tingling with a warning. Nervously I looked out into the black night. There was no moon, no stars, no wind. The air felt heavy, oppressive, muggy and filled with the constant grumbling of thunder.

I thought about the discussion the pilots had had earlier that afternoon; about the U.S. Weather Bureau's diagram of the inside of a cumulonimbus storm cloud, or thunderhead. Of the awesome power and shearing action created within the cloud when air, moisture, debris and what-have-you is sucked upward through the chimney like center. And how in the atmosphere's cold upper reaches, this air and moisture, as it is cooled, becomes heavy and tumbles down the outer fringes of the cloud in the form of hail and severe downdrafts; the hail, sometimes the size of baseballs.

I shuddered just thinking of the number of airplanes and their occupants who over the years have blundered into and have been destroyed by just such boiling monsters.

In the meantime, Margaret Ann is at home rushing around making arrangements for the other kids while we are gone and getting daughter Janet ready to go to the hospital.

I telephone Hulda Purdue on Orcas Island. Hulda was our Orcas reservation taker and local Orcas weather observer. She reports the same indefinite conditions prevailing as at Friday Harbor.

It is only a 30-mile flight to Bellingham from Friday Harbor and I have flown it literally thousands of times in almost every conceivable type of weather... except for tonight's conditions. Out there in that blackness are some real killers. I have tasted their power twice before and I want nothing more to do with them.

My wife and daughter arrive at the airport. For a few minutes I pace the floor, then I call Hulda back, requesting she telephone Thurman Bond. Thurman is a pilot who lives at Doe Bay on the far side of Orcas Island from Hulda and directly under our proposed flight path. Thurman reports having the same conditions as Hulda; very dark, muggy, no wind.

Margaret Ann, Janet and I, in a Cessna 172, depart for Bellingham.

Hulda told me the next day that just minutes after I hung up, she had tried desperately to warn me. Thurman had called back to say that moments after talking to her all hell had broken loose at Doe Bay with screaming winds, hail and lightning.

Margaret Ann and Janet were sitting together on the back seat, Margaret Ann supporting Janet and keeping her wrapped in a blanket. Destination weather was reported as 1,500 overcast, visibility 7 miles, wind calm; thunderstorm activity observed to the west and in the mountain area to the east.

In the inky blackness I could not see the base of the clouds but I knew the ceiling in the Islands was something less than 1,000 feet. Nor could I see the hilly Island terrain which in a number of cases exceeds 1,500 feet, and in one case 2,500 feet. My intention was to fly a flight path as far below the unseen bases of those roiling storm clouds as possible. Consequently we flew at 500 feet, following the crooked and winding channels by memory; blinking reef markers and known house lights confirming the way.

Within minutes of takeoff our invisible propeller-arc turned into an eerie greenish-blue disc of Saint Elmo's Fire. More of the same played along the leading edges of the wings and up and down the windshield. Seeing this, I immediately turned on all the plane's lights to bright; landing lights, cabin lights, instrument panel lights, everything. I also pressed one hand tightly over one eye.

Although I had never experienced it, I was instinctively following the advice of old timers like John Sheasby, "Get the lights on bright, cover an eye. When your plane's friction through the air builds up a sufficiently large static charge, it will discharge from the plane in a blinding white flash. If you are not prepared, you will be blinded... probably long enough to lose control. The covered eye will save you."

We certainly didn't have long to wait. If you can imagine being shot directly in the eyes with a photographer's flash bulb in a relatively dark room... that's fairly close to what this absolutely blinding white light was like. It simply stunned the senses! I do believe, knowledge gained through those 'wasted hours of airplane talk,' (Good God, are airplanes all you guys can talk about?). I think those conversations probably saved our lives that night.

What happened next is hard to describe. It was not raining; visibility was limited for some reason but we were not flying through clouds. It's strange; there was some suggestion of turbulence, a little jerk, a twist, but nothing really substantial to warn of danger. I saw no lightning. One moment we were progressing along satisfactorily, the next instant we were seized! And I do mean seized! I know that isn't much of a description or explanation but that's the way it felt.

We had been flying level. We were still flying more or less level, but the plane with us in it was now rising horizontally at a tremendous rate. This upward thrust with its resultant crushing down pressure on us; the violent tremble and shake of the plane; the noise; hail beating the plane. I don't really know. All I know is we were embroiled in a confusing and terrifying nightmare. A frightening realization seared through my nearly numb brain--- we were being sucked up into the maw of a towering cumulonimbus thunderhead!

My first terrified impulse for survival was to stick the nose of the plane down and dive out of this nightmare. Thank heavens there was still some gray matter functioning and the impulse was cancelled. Any further stress on this little airplane such as a high speed dive in this turbulence and we would be falling to earth in broken pieces.

I was suddenly ringing wet with sweat and my legs were shaking so hard it seemed to take conscious effort to keep my feet on the rudder pedals. Someone was shouting, not screaming, just shouting. My wife said later I was the one who was shouting; such things as "nose up, nose up—too far, damn it too far, steady, steady, don't chase the airspeed, turn right, get away from the mountain, turn right!"

I do and I don't remember that shouting bit, kind of like trying to remember a dream. I do remember tearing one hand free from the controls and frantically trying to brace my head; a terrific shaking was causing the all important instrument panel to be virtually unreadable. I was so scared I figured it must be me doing the shaking.

Scared or not, as a flyer I knew one thing for sure, if I

could not read the attitude gyros, I would lose control and without control my wife and daughter would die with me.

I remember grabbing the instrument panel with one hand and then with the other, of putting my face nearly against the panel, trying desperately to read its message. Everything shook like a bowl of jello; thank God for the new non-tumble attitude gyros, by now the old type would have tumbled and become useless.

Somewhere back there in my numb brain was a crucial piece of information. What was it? Even in this howling madhouse of a situation something kept poking at me. Slowly a glimmer of recall; the falling cold air? Yes! The downdrafts! Besides being sucked upwards, we were still flying forward! Any moment now we would run into a wall of air that would be falling instead of rising!

Good Lord! Would it be possible for this lightly built little airplane of ours to survive such a terrible shearing action? And if we survive it... what then? If our airplane is still in one piece we will pop out through the side of this living hell!

A surge of hope! Almost instantly replaced by a frightening thought... where in God's name was the mountain? Mt. Constitution, 2,500 feet tall... we were flying at 500 feet and approximately three miles away from the base of the mountain when we were snatched. Through these confusing and frightening first minutes or seconds, I could barely keep the aircraft under control, much less maintain a course. Where was that mountain? The altimeter appeared to read 2,000 and winding rapidly upward. The magnetic compass was spinning and unreadable. No way of telling how accurate the gyro compass had remained... but it was that or nothing.

If we have been turning around and around we could ram right into that mountain! Taking a desperate, 'Russian-roulette' type chance on what the blurred image of the gyro was reading, I began fighting the plane around to a course that would hopefully take us away from the mountain.

Suddenly the safety belt nearly knocked the wind out of me! The plane gave an awful screeching grind and then we were falling! Everything loose smashed to the ceiling. For long seconds the restraining belts were the only thing keeping airplane and passengers together. The gasping screams from the back seat made the hair on the back of my neck crawl. With a groaning snap the plane bottomed out and we shot out into the clear. Thank God, there was no mountain in our windshield!

For several moments I felt stunned and confused. How in heavens name could our little airplane, and us, have survived that violence? When the full realization of deliverance dawned... Lord, oh Lord, what a wonderful feeling to be able to breathe again! It was as though we had not drawn a breath since the beginning.

Between fits of roaring static on the radio I was able to hear enough to know that Bellingham Airport was closed, "Heavy electrical storm directly over the airfield... moving from west to east."

Glimpsing the lights of the town of Anacortes through a rift in the clouds, I carefully lined up and started a letdown for the known but unseen channel that runs along Anacortes's waterfront. The clouds were low but thin and the terrain was all low there. As we eased down through the clouds, Anacortes's lights lighted the clouds with a soft and welcoming glow; then we were in the clear! After what we had been through, what a wonderful and friendly sight!

In those days Anacortes had no hospital or airfield. Flying just above the water and under the low cloud base in the narrow channel between Guemes Island and the town, we circled and waited. The reflection of the town lights on the water and on the base of the low clouds was like lights from heaven.

In a very short time Bellingham Radio called us with welcome news— the storm had moved on into the mountains to the east. Flying on the deck, we crept along the mainland's Chuckanut Drive shoreline, below the low hanging clouds and from house light to lighted house. Several times we were startled (and frightened) by sudden rattling hail showers. Our nerves were pretty raw. Finally we came onto the fringes of the city of Bellingham, then the airport.

On arrival at the hospital, daughter Janet was almost immediately given a blood transfusion. As the color crept back into her face the attending nurse said, "your daughter is a very lucky girl!"

My wife looked across the hospital bed at me, a haunted look in her eyes. Neither of us attempted to speak.

CHAPTER 39

The PSA Story

For our flying company, Island Sky Ferries, the years of the '60s were a time for growth and expansion. Our Islands had been discovered. New homes were sprouting up all over the place and these new people were looking for transportation that didn't require hours of waiting, followed by a two-hour ferry ride. Among the new arrivals was the well-known pilot and author, Ernie Gann, who even flew as one of our pilots for several months. Here he is in 1966 giving me a copy of his latest book *In the Company of Eagles*.

Ernie Gann presenting his new book to me

This growth was true throughout most of Puget Sound. Dick Muhlberg, flying his commuter run between

Bellingham and Seattle, was feeling it. Bill Fairchild with his Angeles Flying Service was also feeling it on his runs between Port Angeles and Seattle. The same with Wes Lupien and his Whidbey Flying Service running between Oak Harbor and Seattle; for Bob Crowther flying his Cross Sound Airline between the cities of Bremerton and Seattle and for Tom Wilson's Skyline Air Service, Anacortes to Seattle schedule.

Running daily scheduled flights in and out of a busy, major airport such as Seattle-Tacoma International presented some major challenges for the six of us small operators. None of us were big, rich or influential enough to have our own counter spaces, so we all ended up scattered throughout the passenger Terminal. Crowther ended up using a card table and a chair under the stairwell, the rest of us patched onto whatever airline company was willing, for a few dollars a month, to let our passengers assemble at their counter. These were poor arrangements at best.

Out on the ramp it was just as bad, if not worse. We had no specific area assigned for parking or for unloading and reloading our planes. Here again we ended up scattered here and there… wherever we could make a deal.

I think this whole business of miniature airlines, soon to be called Commuter Airlines, pretty much mystified the Airport Authority. The Authority was certainly aware of us, in fact in conversations with them, it sounded as though they were thinking seriously of asking, not telling us, to go play somewhere else. Our limited financial capacity and yet our volume of welcome, incoming passengers, undoubtedly left them in a quandary.

Wes Lupien, of Whidbey Flying Service, had a great idea. He took it to the Port people and they went for it. They agreed that if Wes would be financially responsible for all six commuters, the Port would assign both a ramp area and a counter area to the group.

Wes formed a little corporation called AIR TAXI INC. and we all joined it. What a difference! We finally had our own counter! People could actually find us! Interline Luggage now came to us instead of us trying to find it! We had a telephone for weather checks and flight plans. We had a luggage belt right to our airplane loading area. As things progressed, Wes soon had women to run the counter and a ramp person to handle the interlining of luggage, etc.

Ah, life was so much better! In fact we pilot/operators, now for the first time, had a chance to sit down over a cup of coffee and talk about things.

This Air Taxi thing of Wes's was working out so well... it opened up all kinds of possibilities. The more we talked about our mutual problems, the more ideas popped up. For example, we were all buying small amounts of ticket stock at high prices. What if, as a group, we bought large amounts? We were all hiring part-time lawyers and accountants who spent very little time putting their minds to our specific problems. Since we were all serving different areas and not competing with each other, what if we as a group hired a full-time lawyer and a full-time accountant?

Well, you can see where this was all leading. Soon we were exploring the possibilities of joining forces; of consolidating our bookkeeping, our maintenance and our routes; of pooling our airplanes and personnel.

As things progressed throughout the summer of 1968, my company and all the other local companies were experiencing the best year ever. One thing led to another. What had been general discussions between us were now gravitating into some serious planning. By the end of the year we were unanimous in our determination to do it. However, when the subject of who would eventually own what, that's when we came to a confused halt. We had no idea of how to equitably split the pot.

The thing was... we had 36 aircraft, all different makes and models— a few new, most old and then older. Some were paid for, most were not. Stirred into this brew was the fact we all owed, to varying degrees, our souls to the "Company Store."

Sure, we all knew how many pilots we would need. We all agreed on how many and what type of airplanes should be used. We knew about schedules. We understood airport fees, the required counter personnel, mechanics, gas boys. We knew about all these things because we were pilots and operational people, not accountants or lawyers. What a problem!

Enter a Mr. Lloyd Douglas. Mr. Douglas lived on my Island and flew frequently on our Seattle flights. Through conversations with Mr. Douglas I learned he was a former accountant who had developed a talent for putting little companies into successful bigger companies. Ah ha! Eventually Mr. Douglas agreed to meet with my fellow operators and me.

He was not thrilled with the numbers we all presented... but he was taken by our enthusiasm!

As 1968 passed into the new year of 1969, we were, per Mr. Douglas's instructions, preparing our companies for certified audits of everything our individual companies owned, owed, leased, used, etc. Property, airports, appraisal of airplanes, engines, engine hours, age of equipment, spare parts, automobiles, chairs, desks, paper, pencils, typewriters, everything would be audited. At the cut-off date, set for June 1, 1969, underground fuel tanks, above ground oil barrels, etc., would be plumbed for verification of gallonage contained; the same for our bank accounts.

This fellow, Lloyd Douglas, was putting everything on a basis that we all understood and accepted. The corporation,

Puget Sound Airlines Inc., (our chosen name) was formed. We would each receive stock in P.S.A. to the value of our contribution.

On June 1, 1969 the six of us relinquished our individual company operating certificates and joined into one company, with its main office in Oak Harbor, Washington and Wes Lupien, President. PSA's Board of Directors was comprised of us, the remaining five former operators.

Backing up a few months, the winter of 1968-69, flying wise, was a veritable bitch. More snow than we had seen in years; howling Noreasters; temperatures below freezing week after week. All of us fighting aircraft icing conditions on almost every flight. Wes telling us about having to lock his arms solid to prevent the control wheel of his plane from moving fore or aft. If it was allowed to move, the ice buildup on the stabilator of his Cherokee Six would cause an overbalance and the plane would plunge dangerously up and down.

The morning of February 5, 1969 was clear and cold. It was the first real weather break we had received in over a month. On this morning, all of us six operators were riding down to Seattle as passengers on our individual morning flights. Dehavilland of Canada was bringing down one of their 20-passenger turbine/propeller powered Twin Otters to Seattle for our perusal. We considered the twin-engined Otter as the number one choice for our soon-to-be-consolidated routes.

After all the weather we had been operating in, now finally we had this beautiful, calm morning and the twin Otter, our dream of dreams was coming. We were all pretty excited!

Shocking, numbing news... Angeles Flying Service's twin-engined Beechcraft, departing Port Angeles for Seattle (Bill Fairchild on board coming to join us) had crashed on takeoff and burned. Bill Booze, my former chief pilot, was flying the plane. Both pilots and their eight passengers were killed.

The cause of the accident was never determined. There was one witness, a mechanic/pilot. He said the airplane on takeoff rotated early and went up steeply. Evidently this was not intentional because the pilot chopped both engines, then immediately slammed them to full power to keep the plane from stalling some 60 or 70 feet in the air. Control was never regained. The plane went up two or three hundred feet, stalled, fell to almost ground level, recovered, went up into another high stall, fell and impacted the ground flat and partially burned.

The plane was 1,200 lbs. under its gross weight. It was loaded properly and was within its annual and 100 hour check. Both engines were delivering full power. The plane's gyrations would indicate the elevator control was jammed. That was never proven. To this day the official National Transport Safety Board report reads, "Causes Unknown."

Bill Fairchild's courageous widow, Mary Lou, representing her company, Angeles Flying Service, joined our group and the preparations for merger continued.

Puget Sound Airlines was not successful. It went into receivership some 18 months later. Why? For a variety of reasons. Ask each of the six of us and you would probably get six different answers.

These are my thoughts on the matter.

As mentioned earlier, 1968 and 1969 were banner years for the whole aviation industry, in fact for the whole country. Load factor for the major airlines was in the high 60s (that means they were averaging two-thirds of their seats full on all flights). So were all of ours.

But then during the winter of 1969-70 the economy started to fall, and so did airline patronage. Other than our little 'Islands to Bellingham' schedule and our old mail run from Anacortes, PSA's income was almost totally derived from interline connections with the major airlines at SeaTac. During this economic slump the major airlines' load factor skidded clear down into the 30s; so did ours.

We (PSA) had planned to sell company stock and most of our hodge- podge of airplanes. We were then planning to standardize on the Dehavilland Twin-Otter to cover our consolidated routes. We even put Pat White, our shop foreman at the time, through the Dehavilland turbine school.

It took us that first summer and fall of '69 to get organized and to get the bugs out of our consolidated operations. By the second summer, 1970, we were ready to make our moves... but by then the economy had really taken a nose dive. It was not the time to sell either stock or airplanes. With no money in reserve and no source of additional capital, with our loads way down and expenses far exceeding our income, we were rapidly getting into big financial trouble.

Another factor that added to our diminishing income— the diversification and drive that had sustained us as individual operators was slowly but steadily fading away.

Fairchild had done glacier flying, flight instruction, supply dropping for the Olympia National Park, and other charter work. His wife, Mary Lou, ran a little airport restaurant. Not an awful lot of money, but enough to subsidize their Seattle run when necessary. PSA wanted to run Seattle schedules, not flight schools or glacier flying (which we knew nothing about). With Fairchild's death these extra income activities ceased.

Lupien, besides his Seattle schedule, had a flight school. The school closed shortly after the merger. Muhlberg in Bellingham, besides his daily Seattle effort, did charter work. That stopped. Crowther in Bremerton, besides a passenger schedule, was involved in freight hauling and Priority Package flying all over the country. Wilson in Anacortes subsidized his infant Seattle schedule with mail hauling and charter work.

My outfit in the Islands, established longer than any of the others, continued on. Besides our Seattle schedule, we had a good paying, seven-day a week passenger and freight schedule to and from Bellingham. We also flew daily utility and County work crews, medical evacuations, law enforcement flights, a daily mail contract and an annual summertime Fire Patrol and supply dropping contract with Mt. Baker National Forest. We also had an aircraft maintenance shop where we not only did our own aircraft maintenance but we took in a fair amount of outside customer work.

The financial situation with PSA was now becoming critical. We had pared down our activities to the point where our only sources of income were the now losing Seattle schedule. My old Island/Bellingham schedule and our traditional Island activities such as the mail contract and the seasonal mountain contract were the only surviving sources of company income.

Wes was president and as we had all previously done as individual owners, the President also held the title of manager. As it turned out, Wes was so busy at Oak Harbor with all the decisions and problems that were flooding in on him that he simply did not have the time or the setup to be forcefully managing the company.

Damn it all anyway, the Board should have recognized that but we didn't. And when Wes would come up with a plan it was often shot down by Board dissension.

For us in Friday Harbor the summer of '69 was a

very busy one. Summers for us in the Islands were always hectic but now in 1969, added to our heavy load of summer passenger traffic and charter demand, we were dispatching for six stations instead of one, and... we were responsible for the maintenance, positioning and dispatching of a fleet of airplanes instead of just our nine. Being the only remaining qualified mountain pilot (after the demise of Fairchild), I was personally tied up on this mountain assignment most of the first and second summers.

Fortunately, our Friday Harbor dispatchers had years of experience. Utilizing my former company's areawide radio network which we expanded to include the new areas of Oak Harbor, Port Angeles and Bellingham, our dispatchers soon had PSA's scheduled flights running efficiently.

In retrospect, what this company really lacked was a hard driving, professional, full-time, overall manager with the power to make decisions and to make them stick. By the time we finally recognized this, it was too late.

During the original formation of PSA I had been sorely tempted to turn in the deed to our airport for what would have been the major block of stock in the new company. Having great expectations for PSA's future, I was afraid I was playing the part of the fool for hesitating and letting this stock opportunity slip by. Many a night I thrashed the pillow over that one.

Finally... even against the advice of Mr. Douglas, I decided we had worked too long and too hard in building that airport to chance the loss of it, so I held it out.

When PSA and the economy started to slip during that first winter of '69-70 (and I became aware of the financial liabilities of corporate directors) I quietly transferred the ownership of our airport to our kids.

A half-year or more later during one of our final meetings, our PSA president, our corporate lawyer and accountant dropped the bomb on the rest of us. Seems we owed money to Uncle Sam (that we didn't have), money we had collected from employees' withholding, etc. Uncle Sam was about to collect from the directors.

That's when the whole Board turned to me and said, "Lucky for us you still have that airport. The rest of us are flat broke. The sale of the airport should just about pay Uncle Sam off."

I stared back at them and eventually said, "But I don't own the airport."

"What do you mean you don't own the airport???"

"No, I don't, the kids own it."

Incredulous stares!

The lawyer cleared his throat, "Ahem... well Roy," he said, "in cases of people owing money to the Federal Government, the Feds can take everything including that which has been transferred within the last five months. When did you-"-- he asked with a little smirk, "transfer the airport ownership"?

I waited a long time before answering. Boy, the crafty, knowing smiles around the table... they were all sure they had me!

"Seven months ago," I answered.

Thank heavens we still had our airport.

CHAPTER 40

The Birth of San Juan Airlines

Prior to going into this ill-fated PSA merger, everything our Air Service owned—the airport, the flying company, the airplanes, the vehicles—everything we had was owned by the corporation, Island Sky Ferries, Inc. Now, still reeling from the traumatic failure of Puget Sound Airlines, I wanted to make sure our stockholders' remaining equity, and mine, was protected as much as possible from the hazards of future adventures.

There had been trouble with the old company name; it did not contain the word 'Airline.' Small companies like ours were now being classified as 'Commuter Airlines.' As our company name began appearing in more and more publications, such as the 'Official Airline Guide,' the word 'Ferries" was raising questions.

After talking it over with our lawyer, Harold Lant, we made the following changes: First (mainly for convenience sake) we shortened the name of the old corporation from Island Sky Ferries Inc. down to its initials, ISF Inc. Secondly, we formed a new flying company named for our County, San Juan Airlines, Inc. (SJA).

Our local bank had loaned us (ISF Inc) their 'maximum allowable' (for the building of our airport)--- so the bank was out of the picture for any further financing. Bob Gregory, friend and bank loan officer, privately went to bat for us.

Gregory was deeply concerned over our County's present lack of air service. He said "What is this community going to do if someone gets hurt and we have no ambulance plane?"

Through his connections and reputation with local Island investors, Gregory raised in three days (in the name of ISF Inc) $110,000. These private investments were secured by a second-place mortgage on the airport (which was fast becoming a valuable asset—and the key to our refinancing).

ISF then used these new funds to buy back our flying equipment from the bankrupt Puget Sound Airlines, Inc. One of our first purchases was the Bushman to cover the daily mail contract and medical evacuations.

Our new corporation, San Juan Airlines, Inc. then leased everything from ISF. This not only included the flying equipment and vehicles (rolling stock) but also the Friday Harbor Airport with all its buildings, facilities, spare parts and equipment.

In this way the flying company (SJA) had no assets other than a bank account; everything was leased. In theory, if an accident occurred, we now no longer had everything in one basket. With insurance covering all of San Juan Airline's liabilities and possible losses (payable to ISF) the airport and the flying operations were finally separated into two different efforts.

Terry Holt (left) and Everett Johnson (right) unloading the mail

Although our (PSA) merger had failed, the need and demand for local air transportation (that we had spent 20 years nurturing) was still here. By the time the spring of 1971 rolled around, our new little company, San Juan Airlines, was scrambling to keep up with the demand.

Our first twin-engine, an Aztec over Friday Harbor

One aircraft we still had was ISF's Cessna 180 seaplane. We sold the airplane's floats to Kenmore and used the 180 as a landplane. The 180 was fine for moving road crews and flying relatively young and agile people, but the plane was too tall for our average daily clientele to climb in and out of. That spring my two sons, Steve and Ken, and I, flew the 180 back to Oklahoma City and traded it in on our first twin-engine—a six-place Piper Aztec. The second spring, 1972, found son Steve and me back in Oklahoma again to buy a second Aztec. The next spring found Dan Weber and me down in Texas trading in one of our Aztecs on a twin-engined, ten-place Britten-Norman 'Islander.' Then it was not more than a year later that we were in California buying a second ten-place 'Islander.'

That reminds me of an interesting winter flight. I call it **The Christmas Story**. It is late afternoon and Christmas Eve. Terry Holt is flying our ten-place twin engined 'Islander' on the Seattle schedule. Terry's 4:00 p.m. northbound flight is fully booked; eight men, one woman, all for Friday Harbor.

The Islander at Orcas Airport

The 4:00 p.m. Bellingham schedule is also booked up.

I've just come in from a local flight and have taken over the dispatch duties from Margaret Ann, giving her a chance to go home and relax a bit before starting dinner. If I know her, the relaxing will amount to loading the washing machine, ironing clothes and cleaning up the house.

Daylight is waning rapidly. We have a temperature of 28 degrees and a low, dark ceiling that smells of snow. It will be totally dark by 4:30 p.m.; earlier if it starts to snow. Consequently all flights are being notified to expedite.

I am not concerned about the Bellingham run. Those pilots are flying visual, below the clouds, and they are much closer to home.

The Seattle run is something else again. It takes 45 minutes to fly it. Seattle's weather is flyable but Terry will have to file an instrument flight plan to get out of there. That means he will be up in the weather. To find our non-instrument equipped airport he will have to find a hole to come down through. . . with falling snow and darkness, that will be difficult.

I telephoned our Seattle counter to inform Terry and the counter personnel of our Island weather situation. I tell the women and Terry, "The instant you have all your passengers checked in, depart. Don't let any of them wander off; every minute you can save down there could mean the difference between landing here or having to return to Seattle."

"Seven of the nine passengers booked have already checked in," they reported.

"Good! Keep track of them, find the other two and load up!"

Not long after talking to Terry it started to snow... and to get dark.

Some 30 minutes later our little Christmas tree and gaily-decorated airport terminal was filling up with happy and expectant islanders. "Did the Seattle flight get away on time? Did everybody show up? Is my husband on board? Did our son make it? When do you expect the flight to get here?"

And from one of our pilots (in a whisper) "there are no holes out there---the ceiling is too low to make a let down---Terry will have to go back to Seattle."

I was banking on one possibility. When I flew in, not too long before, there was a hole over the lighted gravel pit, about a half-mile to the east of our airport.

Another 20 minutes and Terry was on the radio... "I'm on a bearing to Friday Harbor from Whidbey Naval Air Station... We're at 1,500 feet and between layers--- Approaching you now—Don't see any breaks below—Air Traffic Control wants to know my intentions—will have to leave this frequency and refile for Bellingham—or return to Seattle."

"Keep coming Terry," I told him, "Keep coming!"

That's one problem we had with our dispatch being open to the lobby, everyone could hear everything that was said. Believe me, when these people heard Terry say he would have to go back, you could have heard a pin drop, disappointment and concern was written all over their faces.

With finger to lips I cautioned everyone to continue the silence. Pulling the mike cord with me, I stepped out onto the front deck and listened. Soon I could hear the distant pulse of engines.

Terry spoke, "Roy... Air Traffic is getting insistent; where do you want me to take these people?"

"Keep coming Terry, keep coming."

The sound grew. When it was directly overhead I said, "Terry, razz your engines for identification." Lordy oh Lordy, faintly, way up there in the heavens, through that blackness and smother of cloud and snow... I can still hear that sound to this very day... "rrRRrr," "rrRRrr."

"Terry, you are directly overhead... make a 180° standard rate turn to the right."

"WHY?"

"DO IT!"

"OK, OK."

Giving him a moment to establish the turn, I said, (hopefully) "Terry, there is a hole right over the lighted gravel pit—this course will put you right over it."

A moment's hesitation and then Terry answered, "There's nothing... I'VE GOT IT! I'VE GOT IT!" He shouted.

A hundred heart beats or so later, Terry's blazing landing lights cut through the falling snow as he rolled out on final approach to Friday Harbor's runway. The cheers that burst from the expectant Christmas crowd just about took the roof off our little terminal!

By this time we had several inches of snow on the ground. I said to the assembled people, "Go get your cars started... Terry is going to park out at the gas pit... as soon as he stops, turn your lights on and drive out there. Leave your lights on while we unload."

Slipping a jacket on I hurried out to the plane. People were climbing out of cars and the airplane, laughing, hugging, shouting, 'MERRY CHRISTMAS! MERRY CHRISTMAS!"

Terry and I stood for a long moment, just grinning at each other. Then we shook hands and got busy with the luggage.

Terry Holt and Roy with one of our Islanders

CHAPTER 41

Looking Back

By 1979, after 30 some years in the trade, we were no longer young and were definitely wearying of the constant, daily, ongoing scramble. We were thinking seriously of retiring. It would have been nice to turn the reins over to our sons; keeping the flying company in the family, but that did not appear to be in the cards.

Like most small flying companies, our company had no retirement plan. Not only no medical or retirement plan but the company's pay scale had been so marginal over the years that like the rest of our employees, Margaret Ann and I had been literally living from paycheck to paycheck. No stocks or bonds had we.

Between the FAA's new proposed rules and regulations, which were on their way in, the future cost of operations for companies such as ours was going to be much greater. That plus the inevitable economic slump that always follows a boom such as we were then enjoying. And the taking on of an additional debtload to pay off the folks. It was way too 'iffy' for the boys.

The only way Margaret Ann and I could afford to retire was to sell out. Besides... son Ken was bailing out and going the 'big office in the sky' route. This left older son, Steve, less than enthused.

After reading of the challenges and travails we faced over the years in building our small airline, it has probably become obvious to you, and now even to me, that this job had become the dominating factor of my life. I am shocked to find that as I describe these years I find myself mentioning my family so little.

I suppose I can say in defense that the main reason our company survived and eventually prospered, while most others failed, was because of our unceasing attention—like flying and laboring for five years without a break. Perhaps commendable…but at what price to the family?

Yes, those were tough old times and we had to make do with what we had. One thing we did in the winter was to eat our meals at specific times with all family members present. I remember how amazed some of our kids were when they found out that many families did not.

During the summer school vacations when the kids were still quite young, we all spent our summers at the airport. I hope the kids feel the same way, but I don't believe it was all that bad. Since the airport was our summer home, we fixed it up with lawns and flowerbeds. For recreation, we set up an 18-foot swimming pool next to our office/terminal. Our kids and half the town kids had a ball. Later on we had two Volkswagen 'Bugs' and a circular driveway which the kids drove endlessly. Driving-wise, they were restricted to the property but as long as they stayed on the property, almost 'anything went.' The kids all became accredited race drivers. Well maybe not quite accredited but they did become skilled drivers.

I'm sure you understand. Summers were the 'make or break' season for the Air Service. To survive the lean months of the off season, which in those days was everything except summer, we were therefore faced with a frantic yearly summer scramble to gather up and store enough 'acorns' to get us through. To accomplish this required total family dedication— voluntarily or otherwise.

As the family grew, their duties increased. Boys and

girls were mowing lawns, fueling and cleaning airplanes, helping in the Terminal, loading and unloading freight, taxiing airplanes, putting them away, getting them out, helping Mom with the bookwork, washing windows, pulling weeds in the flower beds... and even having fun.

There was nine years age difference between Steven, our oldest and Ken, our youngest. This age difference was pretty handy as far as I was concerned, but it really whizzed Ken off. Here brother Steve was with Dad, probably flying the plane! And Ken was with Mama and the girls; too blankety blank small!

"Just ain't no justice in this life!"

Just like Steve had done, Ken got his Sunday morning turn sitting on my lap and steering. But he wanted me out of there! He wanted the seat to himself just like big brother was doing. Didn't matter whether he could see out or not, it was the principle of the thing, right?

When Steven was 12, he shot, dressed and put his first venison roast on the family table. He was also ready to fly solo. I hadn't realized this... he was just a kid... really coming along, but... he had four years to go before he could legally solo. He evidently thought otherwise. I didn't know that.

He and I were coming back from Bellingham in the old Bushman, empty, one evening. Steve was in the pilot's seat, sitting on a pillow, flying away and holding her as steady as a rock. The old girl's 450 hp Pratt & Whitney engine was out there happily singing her song and swilling gasoline. I thought I'd give the kid a confidence boost so I got up from the co-pilot seat and went back and laid down on the rear hammock seat. The boy never gave any indication of noticing, just casually reached up to the overhead crank and readjusted the plane's trim for my weight shift. I grinned to myself... pretty cool kid!

You are right, those 12 and 14-hour days… and night call outs… they took their toll. I promptly fell asleep. All of a sudden there was no engine noise! I leaped up… That little kid was on final approach to our Friday Harbor runway! Christ! He could hardly reach the rudder pedals and the brakes! You know that kid actually looked disappointed when I slid into the seat next to him and offered to lend a hand!

So I could see this bringing a kid on ' too early' was not a good thing. Many kids that age have the coordination and confidence and it's tough on them when all along they've been encouraged, then told, 'NO!" Of course this new revelation of mine hit the 'little one' doubly hard. There he was, spinning his wheels wanting to do everything his older brother was doing, and now his brother wasn't doing it.

The girls got the short end of the stick. Oh I took them and their friends for airplane rides and two of the three girls eventually grew up to be our bookkeeping department, but none of them learned to fly. They may remember it differently but I don't recall any particular pressure they put on me for flight lessons.

Of course neither you nor I can recreate and relive the identical pressures and circumstances of those days. Trying to recreate all this from the easy chair of retirement is not the same as it was then when every move determined whether there would be beans on the family table or not.

In 1979 we sold San Juan Airlines, Inc. to a Jimmy Sherrill from Oregon. ISF continued to lease the equipment and airport to the new operator.

In 1982 ISF sold the airport to the Port of Friday Harbor. The Port continued to lease most of its airport facilities to San Juan Airlines. The airline soon moved to Port Angeles, Washington. Eventually the airline paid off ISF, and very soon thereafter, 'went broke.'

The Roy Franklin family in 1963
Back row, left to right—Nancy, Steve, Margaret Ann, and Roy
Front row, left to right—Ken, Susan, and Janet

ISF, Inc. was liquidated and its 45 stockholders, or in several cases their heirs, were in turn paid off. A share of ISF stock purchased for $25 in 1956 was worth $500 in 1982. Those who put in $1,000 got back $20,000.

I never did figure it out; $25 for 26 years of compounded interest. Did they do as well or better than what they could have done on the stock market? I hope they did better.

The kids by this time were all off and on their own.

Margaret Ann and I purchased a motor home and hit the high road...

YAHOOOoooooooo Adios!

Chapter 42

Afterword

It is always difficult to write of one's retirement years, about which Douglas McArthur observed that "old soldiers never die, they just fade away." I have not been fading away. My years since selling the Airport and Air Service in 1979 have remained full and interesting. Here are just four vignettes over these years to see if you agree.

The first I'll call *The Cat and I.*

In the back yard curled up on the cab-top of my pickup truck lay my Burmese cat, enjoying as only cats can, the warming rays of an anemic June sun. Walking up to the truck I lay my head down on the pleasantly warm metal beside her. Immediately the rumbling purr of the feline song commenced. Soothed by this song of contentment my mind soon drifted off to another beautiful song, the song of a Pratt-Whitney engine and the rush of wind past my cabin.

Before I had time to get very deep into these nostalgic memories a sudden silence and stiffening of the soft furry body against my cheek snapped me back to reality.

There, passing on the roadway a few feet away from us was a silly Arf Wharf... and was he a sight! Instead of what we consider as normal (belly close to the ground, eyes swinging left and right, tail lashing) there he was, head up, tail up, bouncing along sideways with a silly grin on his face!

It was just too much! My cat and I practically died laughing!

About then a voice from the house called with a message. "The forecast is for rain. If you don't get those beans poled today they are going to be all over the ground!"

"Yes dear, yes dear," I dutifully replied.

I knew the cat was watching me. Slowly I picked up the bean poles and turning I returned the cat's steady stare. Not a sound, not a movement. Suddenly I began prancing around the yard with a silly grin on my face. The cat leaped up and down yowling.

So much for another day of retirement.

The second vignette should not have happened, but I was pushed into it. One day, sometime in about 1980, Ernie Gann decided to drop out of an airplane one day over San Juan Valley. Naturally, I went out to the field to watch, and soon met Joan Lawrence, another elder, who was dressed and ready for a parachute jump herself. She immediately inquired if I was going to jump too. Though I hadn't planned on it and didn't want to, how can this old Navy fighter pilot bow out with any kind of honor left?

So soon I found myself on the jump plane. I had never thought it a good idea to leave a perfectly good airplane.

They say I left fingernail scratch marks clear back to the tail. I swear that is simply a local fable. It was the first parachute jump for all three of us. The picture below shows our survival smiles after our landings. Let's be honest, these were all dual jumps.

Roy with Joan and Ernie after their parachute jumps

Another post-retirement experience has been especially interesting. Our younger son, Ken, and his wife Suzanne have lived on San Juan Island for many years. Ken flies for Fed Ex, and they live on a place in San Juan Valley with their own grass strip. Together they have trained a falcon and worked with the bird in the air over the Island. Ken is an expert jumper, and they set out to find the bird's maximal airspeed. With the help of Todd Roberts, a local pilot, they inserted a microchip on the falcon's tail to measure airspeed, and developed through computer simulations the most aerodynamic shape for a lure with food for the bird.

I had the fun of flying the jump plane, a souped-up 172, over the Valley for their training flights and drops with the drop zone over the south end of the Island near American Camp. The culmination of the project was a flight in 2003, when the falcon achieved a top speed of 209 miles per hour after Ken released the lure. This was captured on film in the air by Norman Kent, a photographer/jumper working with the National Geographic Society. The bird just pulled in its wings more and streaked past Ken to catch the food. This has gone on to a Disney movie to be shown soon across the country.

Roy in the jump plane

Ken (right) with the internationally known jumper/photographer, Norman Kent (left)

In September of 2005, I was honored to have the new Terminal at Friday Harbor Airport named after me. At the time of turnover of the airport to the Port of Friday Harbor in 1979, there had been a movement in the community to name the airport Roy Franklin Field. I had resisted that at the time, feeling that Friday Harbor Airport was just fine as is. The dedication day for the Terminal was special for me in many ways. Many of my old friends were there, including Bob

Nichols, Terry Holt, Fred Sundstrom, and others who had helped make all of this possible. Another special treat was to see the good old Bushman again. I had sold the airplane to Bill Helsell some years ago. I had known Bill in primary flight training in the Navy way back in the early 1940s. He now lives in Seattle, hangars the plane in Everett, and was good enough to fly her up for the occasion.

Roy with banner at dedication of Friday Harbor's
Roy Franklin Terminal on September 10, 2005

Roy with an old friend at the Dedication ceremony

Closing out this story, it has been a privilege to have lived through interesting times and to share this journey with you. Unfortunately, some of those to whom I owe so much are no longer with us, including Cap and Virginia Ferris, Bob Schoen, Bill Booze, Dan Weber, Bill Savage, and Bob Faucett. Many others are still going strong. Fred Sunstrom, who did all of the bulldozing for the airport over 40 years ago, still lives on San Juan Island. Terry Holt is my next-door neighbor, and delivers motor homes and trailers all over the country. Bob Nichols is retired and living with his wife in Ephrata, Washington. Dick Palmer is retired in Bellingham.

As I said in an earlier chapter, I was worried that the many years of around-the-clock work, often seven days a week, had taken too big a toll on my family. This treasured letter, written to me for Father's Day in 1977 by Susan, our oldest daughter, goes a long way towards providing some comfort in that area.

Dear Dad,

Last night Kenny and I were reminiscing about our early childhood. It suddenly occurred to me that at about the same age as Steve and I are, you and Mom were struggling to build an airport out of the woods. Kenny was either too young to remember, or hadn't even been born yet... so I started telling him of my memory of myself as a little girl, climbing over fallen trees, struggling behind Mom in the hot sun to bring you a jar of cold water and a sack lunch. The sun and the smell of the fallen trees, the insects making their crackling little sounds, and the birds chattering everywhere, is as vivid in my mind as if it happened yesterday. It seemed so simple and obvious then... my Dad's building an airport... no big deal!

Good grief, would any of us have the guts to do such a thing now? To take acres of nothing but woods and boulders, carve out a landing strip, building sites, roadways--- from scratch!!

We've entered into such an entirely different stage of life. Not many people take big chances anymore... not unless they have plenty of money to back them up. You and Mom had nothing... except five children (give or take one or two depending on the time!)

All of this just to tell you how much I admire you for your dreams and hopes and how you have seen them through. You have you know... you have a grown family working in the business that was only a dream when they were small children. You've nurtured their love of this Island, of the land, and of the profession you're proud of.

I've tried to do the same for my children. "Stop! Smell that beautiful woodsy smell! Oooo... it's sooo good!"

They probably sometimes think I'm crazy... but I know they'll remember and love me for it later.

You've come a long way in your business and I'm sure there's a long way to go yet. Somehow though it's sad, because it's no longer hopes and dreams... it's politics. In some ways I'd like to see you and Mom "take your memories and run." I'd really like to see you be able to have the time, and the energy, to enjoy each other; your land, travel, etc.

So, whatever happens in the next couple of years to affect the Company... I hope you will realize that at least to me, you have accomplished it all. And more some!

This is a long winded way of saying... thanks for the memories and... Happy Father's Day!

With love, from your oldest daughter,
Susan

The airport and airline were a family affair all the way. Margaret Ann was a mainstay from start to finish. The girls helped a lot in the business side of our operations, and both Steve and Ken flew for the Airline at one time or another. It has been gratifying to see both of our sons pursue a career in aviation, even after seeing the travails of their old Dad over the years. Four of our five children still live on San Juan Island. Steve lives in Long Beach, California, where he owns and operates Catalina Flying Boats, a successful air freight business. The Franklin family now includes nine grandchildren and two great grandchildren.

As you learned in earlier chapters, we sold the flying company to Jim Sherrill of Oregon in 1979, and at the same time leased the airport to the Port of Friday Harbor. Three years later the Port, with the help of Federal funds purchased the airfield from us and developed and expanded it into the fine facility that it now is. Margaret Ann and I bought a motor home and spent the next 20 years exploring the North American Continent from Alaska to California, from the Pacific Ocean to the Atlantic.

Our final trip together

It has been lonely since Margaret Ann passed away from cancer in 2001. This journey would not have been possible without her at my side all the way. I have been blessed with a wonderful family, colleagues, and friends and have had a rich experience. I would do it all over again, though another time would not have to be quite so interesting as this journey was!

About the Author

Roy Franklin flew for the first ongoing flying service in the San Juan Islands in the late 1940s. He bought the company called Island Sky Ferries Inc. in 1953. Persevering against adversities of weather, lack of navigational aids, and initial lack of facilities, he operated a safe and effective commuter airline for the next 26 years.

Roy was raised on a farm near Ferndale, Washington. He flew fighters in the U.S. Navy during World War II. After the war, he moved to San Juan Island in 1948 to continue his flying career. His wartime experience flying Wildcats off of jeep carriers soon proved useful in flying from dirt strips on our Islands.

Island Sky Ferries operated for the first ten years from a cow pasture on Lyle King's ranch in San Juan Valley. The Airline bought 64 acres on the present airport property in 1954, then put all their efforts, savings, and bank loans to work in clearing land and establishing the airport. The new airport was opened in 1959, with two runways (2,300 and 1,300 feet). Roy built the first terminal, maintenance shop and hangars on the new airport. Lights were added in the 1960s. Passengers and freight were flown on daily flight schedules throughout the San Juan Islands, to and from Bellingham and Seattle. Also charter flights for whatever needs arose, including all kinds of emergencies. Despite the many adversities of this early "bush flying," not one passenger was ever injured over 30 years of scheduled air service.

Roy sold the Airline, now named San Juan Airlines in 1979. He sold the airport to the Port of Friday Harbor in 1981. Although many people at that time wanted the airport to be named Franklin Field, Roy asked that the field retain the town name, Friday Harbor Airport. Roy has remained active in flying since the 1980s, and has continued to make important contributions to aviation in this area. He has lived on San Juan Island continuously for the last 58 years. His dedicated and long-term contributions to aviation and public service in the San Juan Islands over the years were recognized in 2005 by naming the new Friday Harbor Airport Terminal in his name and establishing a Museum there to honor his and others' years of service to these Islands.

The author in 1993

Made in the USA